INTRODUCTION TO
THEATER

INTRODUCTION TO
THEATER
A DIRECT APPROACH

LAURIE J. WOLF

Library of Congress Control Number:		2012918768
ISBN:	Hardcover	978-1-4797-2945-6
	Softcover	978-1-4797-2944-9
	Ebook	978-1-4797-2946-3

This book was printed in the United States of America.

Photograph by Geoffrey Wade
Rhinoceros, February 2011
Actors: Zoe V Speas, Greg Benson

To order additional copies of this book, contact:
Xlibris Corporation
1-888-795-4274
www.Xlibris.com
Orders@Xlibris.com
118929

CONTENTS

INTRODUCTION

WHEN I BEGAN to write this book, I sat back and tried to remember all of the theatre history texts that I have had to read (and suffer through) during all the years I was an undergraduate, postgraduate, and now, even as I assign the material. I tried to determine what worked for me and what did not. The conclusion I came to was that there was a surfeit of fluff that went into the production of most theatre textbooks, even if they were Introduction to Theatre books. It is one thing to sit down and read your assignment; it is quite another to wade through pages and pages of extraneous material that are basically repeating the same information over and over.

With this book, I decided to try to do away with the repetition, to think about who the audience actually is and what information does one need to know at this level. There are certainly enough books out there should you decide to pursue the art of theatre further. In the meantime, try out this book, and see if you like the technique of getting straight to the point.

Happy reading.

CHAPTER 1

WHAT IS THEATRE?

WHEN IT COMES to theatre and performance, it may seem, to the uninitiated, like a different world: full of new languages, ideas, and constructions. There are a multitude of definitions for both terms. Theatre has often been defined as (1) the space for performance, (2) writing that is suitable for dramatic presentation, (3) a building designed for the performance of plays and (4) a room for performing surgical procedures. As you can see, the possibilities are many and varied.

What exactly are the conditions needed for theatre? There needs to be an actor/performer and an audience. Theatre is about an exchange of ideas, about helping us to understand our place in the world. Theatre mirrors and influences its society's view of the world: its history, philosophy, religious attitudes, social structure, theoretical assumptions, ways of thinking about humanity, and the world and nature. It structures our understanding of experience and gives us a means by which to process it.

Watercube, Beijing, China, Bryan Allison, 2008

What is the definition of drama? Literally, the word comes from the Greek, meaning "to do" or "to act." What is drama in relation to theatre? If theatre is the exchange of ideas, then drama is the means by which they are exchanged. Why is drama so essential? What are its uses, its aims? There are some who advocate that drama helps to develop a sense of worth and encourages creativity and imagination. This is true but does not make the term any less elusive. Often, the first thing that is asked in an Introduction to Theatre course is the definition of the word "drama." Generally, the class will not respond, pretending to be deep in thought, but in reality, they are calling upon the gods for divine inspiration. Initially, it seems a natural enough question, but in reality, the answer is anything but simple. Some people think of drama as a gritty television show. For others, drama means the works of Sophocles, Euripides, and Aeschylus, or Tennessee Williams and Arthur Miller. One way to describe drama is through the idea of representation and its role in the identification and dissemination of meaning.

The definitions for performance have their own parameters. The theorist Richard Schechner states that nearly any activity can be seen as performance. He qualifies that statement by breaking it down into methods of perceiving an activity. As an example, he suggests a sporting event, such as the Olympics. Not only are the opening and closing ceremonies hugely theatrical, but also the whole nature of the competition is one of showmanship—there is a performer(s) and there is an audience. The particular competition is the performance, and the sense of nationalism that pervades the event is the discourse that gives meaning to the occasion.

One of the things that Schechner says about performance is that one needs to understand the difference and relationship between "is" and "as" performance. Generally, we say that something "is" or "was" a performance (e.g., a lecture or the resignation of a president) when it is preplanned. "As" performance is a way of studying the world seen "from the perspective of" or "in terms of." An example of this is an operating theatre. There is clearly a star—the surgeon—and additional actors, the patient and others in the surgical suite. If the operation is occurring in a teaching hospital, there is even an audience in the gallery.

Who or what is needed to create theatre? There is not a single "thing" or person, but rather a whole group of people—actors, director, designers, technicians, and of course, the audience. Theatre is a collaborative art, and it cannot happen without the cooperation of these many and varied people.

Collaboration implies people working together as a unit and is predicated on that unit functioning successfully by means of mutual respect.

Audience for Richard Stallman's Talk at Teatro Alvear, Beatrice Murch, 2009

The Audience

When watching a performance, you experience a number of phenomena simultaneously. For one, theatre is a group experience. Although the people who make up the crowd of theatregoers are themselves individuals, once they have become a "crowd," they begin to think with a "collective mind which makes them feel, think, and act in a manner quite different from that in which each individual would feel, think, and act were s/he in a state of isolation."

All groups are different. Some are aggressive, like an angry mob; others are generally more subdued, like passengers on public transport. A crowd at a sporting event is very different from a group at a religious function, and the crowd that composes a theatre audience is still very different from any of these examples.

Another phenomena experienced by the collective audience is the feeling of *empathy*. Empathy is the emotion that is generated when you emotionally identify with another person and his situation. It is the capacity for putting yourself in someone else's shoes and understanding (and sometimes feeling) what they are experiencing. In the theatre, it refers to a sense of recognition of something in one of the characters; it is not the same thing as sympathy, although you may experience that as well. Empathy is when you feel along with the characters—it provides a sense of participation in the play for the audience. Have you ever screamed at the scariest parts of a horror movie? Have you ever felt your body react as a character's on the screen, as they jump or try to run away? This is an empathetic response, and in the theatre, this response is stronger because you are sharing it with live performers and other members of the audience.

Aesthetic distance is the psychological separation or sense of detachment that an audience experiences. It is what (usually) keeps the audience under control and from shouting out responses to the stage (unless specifically invited to do so). The audience understands that what is happening on the stage is not real; that eventually, the lights will come up, they will leave, the actors will change out of costume and makeup and become ordinary people again.

Aesthetic distance allows you to critically assess the performance that you just viewed, evaluate the performers, and make judgments, either positive or negative, about various design elements.

In recent years, there have been numerous productions that have invited audience participation. This sort of direct participation calls for a completely different type of audience interaction. Rather than being an unobserved spectator who is sometimes directly addressed from the stage but who bears no responsibility for response, the audience is specifically focused upon and requested to join the action. In these situations, the audience is encouraged to relate to the actor as an actor, rather than as the character.

One of the tropes that is often used when talking about the theatre is "the willing suspension of disbelief." This was a phrase that was coined by Samuel Taylor Coleridge in the early nineteenth century. It means—for our purposes, in talking about the theatre—that while we know what is happening on stage is fictional, we will ignore that knowledge for the period of the play and accept the action and characters as if what was happening was real; this requires a leap of the collective imagination of the audience.

We use our imagination in many different ways each and every day. In daily life, we use symbols to make meaning; for example, this process of carrying meaning depends on the use of codes that may be the individual sounds or letters that humans use to form words, the body movements they make to show attitude or emotion, or even something as general as the clothes they wear.

Dreams present another case demonstrating the potential of the imagination. You may have the most exhilarating dream that you are flying through the air; then, when you awake in your own bed, you find that the dream carries more significance to you than the reality of your bed. As a result of the work of Sigmund Freud (1856-1939) on the subconscious, people tend to accept the value and the "reality" of dreams, nightmares, and symbols in the human mind.

Although theatre is not real in a literal sense, it can appear to be real in an emotional or intellectual way. As an art form, theatre can oftentimes be more truthful about life than a routine, detached narrative.

In this chapter, we have examined the nature of theatre and drama, the imagination and the role of the audience; however, there are many different factors that play a large part in the overall theatrical experience. In the next chapter, we will examine the role of the actor, and the stage spaces in which s/he may perform.

For Further Reading:

Colin Counsell and Laurie Wolf. *Performance Analysis*. London: Routledge, 2001.

Daniel Gerould, ed. *Theatre/Theory/Theatre: The Major Critical Texts from Aristotle and Zeami to Soyinka and Havel*. New York: Applause, 2000.

John Harrop and Sabin R. Epstein. *Acting with Style*. Boston: Allyn and Bacon, 2000.

Richard Leacroft and Helen Leacroft. *Theatre and Playhouse*. London: Methuen, 1984.

CHAPTER 2

ACTING AND THEATRE SPACES

Procession of Characters from Shakespeare plays by unknown
British artist, circa 1840

A T THE MOST basic level, every human is an actor. Every person
performs social roles for others, both consciously and unconsciously.
This is not a pejorative statement; it is merely a fact. Psychologists and
psychiatrists from Sigmund Freud onward have explored the role-playing of
the human being in order to better understand behavior, to assess internal
conflicts, and to treat emotional problems. Major playwrights and other
writers of fiction from Aeschylus and Euripides (fifth century BCE) among
the ancient Greeks to contemporary playwrights such as Caryl Churchill
(b.1938) and Tony Kushner (b.1958) have continually explored the ways
in which people pretend to be someone they are not or profess to believe
something other than reality for purposes that are useful or detrimental,
economic or religious, comic or tragic. We know that people perform
different roles when interacting with different friends, acquaintances,
family members and strangers. Think about how you interact with the
different people in your life. Do you act the same way around everyone?
Probably not. People perform differently in private situations than they do
in public. Social behavior is a fundamental aspect of human interaction and
is essential to the dramatic content and conflict of the theatrical experience.
It is surprising then that an early Greek word for actor is *hypocrites*, from
which we derive the negative words "hypocrisy" and "hypocrite."

As early as the fourth century BCE, Aristotle identified *mimesis* or
what has come to be known as art imitating life. Children are constantly

role-playing and often use imitation as a means of learning to understand the world around them. All of us probably engaged in some form of make believe early in life. By the time we have matured, although some of this activity continues, of course, it often occurs in more controlled, private ways or perhaps during the social freedom of a costume party. Participation in theatrical production gives consent to this sense of play.

For those who choose acting as a profession, the practice of *mimesis* goes beyond the act of copying and into the realm of creating and developing characters from the observation and analysis of living models and from a close exploration of self. What the actor eventually presents to an audience is a truthful picture of a character, although the playwright devises the words, someone else (the director or choreographer) has instructed her/ him how to move, and the actor's own set of beliefs and actual behavior is hidden from the audience.

Tibbits Opera House Proscenium, P.A. Jamison

Space

All you need for drama is a space. An empty space. Think of empty spaces, or "arenas," that are used for staging events:

- Concert hall
- Sports stadium
- Circus ring

Now consider some questions that could apply to all of these spaces and potential activities that would take place therein. What do they have in common? How is the audience arranged? What is the relationship between the audience and the performers? Is the audience involved in the action? How? Why?

For an event to be considered a theatrical performance, it must take place in a venue that has the capacity for both the performers and the audience. The space could be miniscule (e.g., a closet with a single actor performing for a single member of the audience) or the performance area could be the size of a studio sound stage, as it was in director Peter Brooks's 1985 heroic retelling of *The Mahabharata*, the greatest, longest and one of the two major Sanskrit epics of ancient India, the other being the *Rāmāyana*.

It is vital that the space be arranged with the movement of the actors and their relationship to the audience as top priority. Although theoretically, the physical possibilities are wide open, there are several spatial configurations that have become traditional in the past 2500 years. These traditional spaces—proscenium, thrust and arena—are defined largely by the physical relationship of the performers to the audience. Environmental staging takes a different approach to the actor/audience dynamics all together.

Proscenium Stage

The proscenium stage consists basically of a platform behind a permanent opening (proscenium arch). Usually a curtain can be lowered or a pair of curtains closed and so separates the stage from the auditorium. Even when the curtains are open, there is a sense that the stage and the audience are in different spheres; the audience is looking through a "picture frame" into another world. This disconnection is further augmented by the addition of the orchestra pit, which is present in many theatres.

The disadvantage of this separation of audience and performers is exactly that division—it tends to lead to a forced or artificial method of acting. On the other hand, it has the advantage of allowing realistic scenery to be constructed on the stage with elaborate effects. This form of stage space was conducive to the genres of theatre known as Naturalism and Realism, which will be discussed in later chapters. Although this type of theatre was very popular for many years, and still is, there is no reason to believe that this style is any more "correct" than any other stage space.

National Museum of Scottland Street Theater Performance,
opening ceremony, Brian McNeil, 2011

Thrust Staging

In 1576, the first building designed specifically for the performance of plays was erected in London for actor, James Burbage (1531-1597). It was a wooden circular building and open to the weather. It copied many of the features of an inn yard; there were galleries around it from where the rich could watch the plays, and the stage thrust out from one wall into the middle of the area where ordinary people stood. This building was called "The Theatre."

The audience surrounds this type of thrust stage on three sides. The main advantage of this is that the actors are not separated from the audience; they are in the midst of them. It is easy for an actor to make an "aside" directly to the audience, and soliloquies can be spoken naturally, as though the speaker is sharing her/his thoughts privately with those immediately adjacent.

The thrust stage has an advantage over arena staging; there is a back wall, which can serve as a piece of permanent scenery. In addition, it has the intimacy and immediacy, which is a feature of theatre-in-the-round.

Arena Staging

Many modern theatres are designed so that the stage is "in-the-round." What are the advantages and/or problems of staging a play in such a configuration? As soon as you begin performing in an arena space, there is much greater intimacy. The spectators are close to the action and become much more engaged. It is as if they are eavesdroppers, glimpsing a world that is going on in the midst of them. In arena staging, actors are able to relate to each other and do not need to project to the audience, as the audience is *right there*.

Arena staging discourages the use of much scenery; it promotes the practice of minimalistic or stylized staging, set pieces that are emblematic rather than realistic or descriptive. This method of staging also reinforces aesthetic distance; because the audience is able to see other audience members also watching the performance, it serves to remind the audience that they are viewing a production and not a substitute for real life.

Nontraditional Theatre Spaces

A nontraditional or "found" theatre space can be anywhere, outside or inside; the main prerequisite is that it was not originally intended as a performance space when it was designed. A production company may find a space that is appropriate for the particular play they wish to produce, and it may be a space that was never intended for performance. The venue might be used as it is discovered or undergo some sort of modification, but the important point to remember is that any space may become a theatrical location, whether it is a church, factory, school, café, street corner, or mountainside.

Whichever type of theatre space is used for any individual play, it must be appropriate to the needs of the production—the genre, the story, the style of acting, and what type of response the director and playwright are hoping to achieve from the audience. There will be times when the director must fit the production to the space, which s/he is given; other times, there will be more flexibility, and the production may grow to fill the space.

For Further Reading:

Richard H. Palmer. *The Lighting Art: The Aesthetics of Stage Lighting Design.* New York: Allyn and Bacon, 1993.

Robert Edmond Jones. *The Dramatic Imagination: Reflections and Speculations on the Art of the Theatre.* New York: Routledge, 2004.

Gay McAuley. *Space in Performance: Making Meaning in the Theatre.* Ann Arbor: University of Michigan Press, 2000.

Marvin Carlson. *Places of Performance: The Semiotics of Theatre Architecture.* Ithaca: Cornell University Press, 1993.

W. Oren Parker and R. Craig Wolf. *Scene Design and Stage Lighting.* Fort Worth, Tex.: Harcourt Brace, 1996.

Theater at Epidaurus, Fingalo, 2007

CHAPTER 3

TEXTUAL ANALYSIS

O NE OF THE earliest tasks that must be undertaken when preparing for a production is selecting the play that is going to be produced. Whether it is a classical play (perhaps a play by Sophocles or Shakespeare), a contemporary play (something by Arthur Miller or Marsha Norman) or a brand new work, there are certain steps that must be taken before the script is ready to be handed over to the actors and worked on in rehearsal. The director needs to analyze the text and develop a concept surrounding the material—this is a complex procedure and one, which will be discussed in detail in a later chapter, that addresses the role of the director.

There are very specific points to look for as you approach a script. Reading a dramatic text is a particular discipline. One of the most important points to bear in mind, no matter the historical period the play is from, is that dramatic texts were written for performance before an audience, not to be read quietly to oneself. Why is this important? A piece of writing that is not meant for performance may be written in a narrative, third person voice; a piece written for the theatre occasionally has a narrator, but is more likely to be made up of dialogue between a variety of different characters. There is action that can be seen and emotion that is expressed. The text is actually no more than a transcript, a scenario. Shakespeare, for example, seemed to have paid no attention to the publication of his plays; he put his energies into having them seen, heard and understood in performance.

Antigone and the Body of Polynices-Project Gutenberg, eText 14994

This idea applies even further to the Greek dramatists of fifth century BCE. The playwrights would instruct the chorus and actors—he acted as both director and producer. In this situation, his job did not end with the script but with the performance.

When you read any script, especially one that carries the weight of history with it, you need to be aware that the written quotation of any spoken sentence is a very incomplete transcript of what was conveyed verbally. When you read a text, you miss the tone of voice, nuance, pace, stress, facial expression, gesture and physical posture, and positioning of the actor. More importantly, the script alone does not convey the roles and social or personal relationships of the characters involved, their past or their shared assumptions. It is missing that all-important context.

What do we need to look at in order to contextualize any dramatic text that we read? It is important to remember that theatre does not happen in a vacuum: it is influenced by the cultural, social and political milieu of its day. As such, it can be read as an artifact of its own time and the dramatic text is an example of that.

How does the playwright communicate? The media of the playwright are the bodies and the voices of his actors. It is essential that we understand the magnitude of an audience. As I explained in chapter 1, their shared experience is part of the play as a whole; the performance was designed to take the thoughts and emotions of the audience along with it. The ideal situation is to see and hear a theatrical piece in a considered and informed manner.

Bust of Aristotle. Marble, Roman copy after a Greek bronze original by Lysippos from 330 BCE, Jastro W., 2006

Play for Study: Sophocles's Antigone

Antigone is the third of the three Theban plays, written around 442 BCE. The Theban Trilogy consists of *Oedipus Rex (Oedipus the King)*, *Oedipus at Colonus*, and *Antigone*, but the play considered the last of the three was, ironically, written first. Only seven of Sophocles's tragedies have survived to the modern era—with the trilogy surviving the ages intact. These three plays are perhaps the most famous of the seven, with *Antigone* performed most often.

Antigone tells the story of the title character, daughter of Oedipus (the former king of Thebes, who unknowingly killed his father and married his mother, and who renounced his kingdom upon discovering his actions), and her fight to bury her brother Polyneices against the edict of her uncle, Creon, the new king of Thebes. It is a story that pits the law of the gods—"unwritten law"—against the laws of humankind, family ties against civic duty and man against woman.

Many playwrights in Ancient Greece used mythological stories to comment on social and political concerns of their time. This is what Sophocles may have intended when he wrote *Antigone*. Based on the legends of Oedipus, Sophocles may have been trying to send a message to the Athenian general, Pericles, about the dangers of authoritarian rule.

These tragedies were written to be performed at the Great Dionysia (a festival in honor of the god Dionysus, the god of fertility, theatre, and wine) in Athens. Attending these plays was considered a civic duty, and even criminals were let out of jail to attend. *Antigone* won Sophocles first prize at the festival and was an enormous success. It is still performed today; a noted production was the adaptation by French playwright Jean Anouilh, who set the play during World War II.

As stated previously in this chapter, it is important to understand the cultural referents of the play under scrutiny. In the case of the *Antigone*, it is important to not only understand a number of conventions of Greek theatre, but it is helpful to appreciate the dramatic world from which the play was produced. For example, in Greek tragedy, violence occurs offstage and is only reported. There were only three actors and a chorus of twelve, and men wearing masks played all the parts.

In a play like *Antigone*, it is useful to have some knowledge of the role of women and the family. The Athenian family group, called the *oikos*, was considered to be a living organism, which had to be renewed every generation in order to remain a vital life form. The organization of the city-states required that kinship, especially of citizens, be legally defined. The rules of inheritance meant that preference was given to direct lineal heirs, which guaranteed that a child born out of wedlock had no kinship rights or claims to property. During the reign of Pericles, if the mother was not an Athenian citizen, the child was automatically considered to be illegitimate.

The place of the well-born woman was in the home. Less well-to-do women worked outside of the home, but they really just did jobs that were the same as those they did at home; they worked as washerwomen, woolworkers, midwives, and the like. Within the geography of the house, the woman's place was inside and in the back, whereas the men's location was on the street side of the house.

If you begin to put this information together with the text of *Antigone*, it is possible to see how greatly she transgressed the traditions of her world. First of all, she antagonized Creon, the king, which, as anyone knows, is not the smartest thing to do. Next, in order to bury her brother, Polyneices, she was continually seen out in public, something that was not looked on with favor for women of a certain social standing and certainly not for a woman of the royal family. Furthermore, she was an active participant in the dramaturgy, or dramatic composition, of the play.

This brings us to the topic of *dramatic structure*. This is a model that was suggested by the philosopher Aristotle in the fourth century BCE. It is the earliest surviving work of dramatic structure and for all intents and purposes held its position until well into the twentieth century when theorist and playwright Bertolt Brecht offered a significant alternative (more on Brecht and his theories in chapter 11).

Aristotle wrote his *Poetics* (which focused upon the art of Drama) in two parts: Tragedy and Comedy. The section on comedy is now lost, but the writings on tragedy survive in a good amount of detail. Aristotle divides the elements of tragedy into six parts:

- **Plot**—Aristotle says, "Tragedy is not an imitation of men but of actions and of life. It is in action that happiness and unhappiness are found, and the end we aim at is a kind of activity, not a quality." In other words, he is saying that the plot is the end for which tragedy exists, and that end is the most important thing of all.
- **Character**—When talking about character, Aristotle suggests that there are four aims to be achieved:

- First and foremost, the characters shall be good
- The characters shall be appropriate
- The characters should be lifelike
- They need to be consistent

This may seem obvious, but do not forget that we have been influenced by the writings of Aristotle for the past 2,500 years.

The third point of Aristotle's model is:

- **Thought**—"Obviously, in their actions as well as in their utterances, the personages will employ Thought in these same categories whenever they have to inspire pity or terror or convey a sense of importance or plausibility simply by impression immediately without verbal expression."
- **Language**—Aristotle goes into the lexical technicalities of language but for our purposes, what is important is that language concerns forms of expression.
- **Melody**—Aristotle believed that the chorus was an integral part of the performance and should share in the action.
- **Spectacle**—He left spectacle for last because he thought that if a production had beautiful costumes and scenery but a bad script and acting, there was something wrong with the play. We tend to think in similar ways today; if you leave a play talking about the scenery, then something significant was missing from the performance.

Returning to standard dramatic structure, the basic shape came from Aristotle's suggestion that each *episode* of dialogue or *stichomythia* be interspersed by a choral ode. This idea has developed in this way: the play begins with an *exposition*. This is where a good amount of the backstory is told. Many times, there is a delayed exposition and we find out pieces of information along the way, but in a traditional Naturalistic or Realistic play, the greater part of the information is revealed here.

The exposition leads to the *rising action*, where the main action begins to unfold and where secondary plots start to reveal themselves. This is also where conflicts and obstacles begin to arise for the protagonist. These tensions lead to small crises along the way until the major *climax* occurs. This is the turning point of the story, the moment where there is no going back. If the play is a comedy, it is likely that events will start to turn in the direction for the protagonist. If it is a tragedy, events will probably only get worse.

Following the climax is the *falling action*. This is where the conflict between the protagonist and antagonist begins to resolve itself; there may be another point of suspense during which the outcome of the conflict is in doubt. The last section of this structure is the *dénouement*, the wrapping up of loose ends, and the conclusion.

This is a conventional dramatic structure; however, there are many other structures to be found. In Shakespearean drama, for instance, the climax tends to occur in the third act, but there are two additional acts with action that can rarely be classified as "falling action." Many contemporary plays do not follow the traditional pattern either. Feminist writers tend to deviate from this style, seeing it as a representation of patriarchal oppression in writing; the result is that both feminist and women's writing in general tends to be more malleable in terms of space and time—it does not necessarily follow a strict cause to effect configuration.

In this chapter, we have started to examine the necessary elements in order to begin the analysis of a dramatic text. We have applied these ideas to Sophocles's *Antigone* and looked briefly at the *Poetics* by Aristotle. We have also looked at some length at the traditional paradigm of dramatic structure. In the next chapter, we will continue to look at elements of dramatic structure, examine the role of the director and apply these aspects when approaching a play for performance.

For Further Reading:

David Ball. *Backwards and Forwards: A Technical Manual for Reading Plays.* Carbondale: Southern Illinois University Press, 1990.
J L Styan. *The Elements of Drama.* Cambridge: Cambridge University Press, 1960.
Ronald Hayman. *How to Read a Play.* New York: Grove Press, 1999.
Willmar Sauter. *The Theatrical Event: Dynamics of Performance and Perception.* Iowa City: University of Iowa Press, 2000.

CHAPTER 4

ROLE OF THE DIRECTOR

T HE DIRECTOR IS the most prevailing force in a production, yet is one of the last aspects of which a general audience is aware. However, the person taking on this role is accountable for all creative aspects of a production. It is that person's responsibility to interpret the script, to see that what happens on stage reflects the author's intentions; to understand the play—its plot, structure, characterization, background, and themes; to visualize the play; to audition, select, rehearse, and guide the actors; to link the work of the designers, technicians, and stage management; to keep within budget; to maintain a workable schedule; and to provide the audience with as high a standard of entertainment as possible.

The director is a relatively new role in the theatre. Although the function of direction occurred (e.g., Aeschylus directed his own plays and Greek choruses were directed by the chorus leader), in fact, throughout theatre history, there are numerous instances of plays being directed by the playwright or a performer or stage manager. However, it can be difficult to produce a consistent production when there is not an individual who holds a single, cohesive vision for the performance.

Historically, it was unusual for an actor to have a complete script during rehearsals. Think about the 1998 film *Shakespeare in Love*. As the character of Shakespeare was writing *Romeo and Juliet*, none of the actors (nor the producers, for that matter) knew what the play was about. When the egotistical actor, Ned Alleyn (Ben Affleck) arrived, Shakespeare convinced him to act in the play by telling him that the play was called *Mercutio*. The "actors" in the play were given "sides"—just a small section of script with a line or two from another character and then their own lines. As you can imagine, when this is done in real life, how difficult it is to produce a well-structured and coherent performance.

George II Sachsen-Meiningen

It is often stated in theatre history texts that the theatre director did not exist prior to 1874, when a German nobleman, Georg II (1826-1914), Duke of the Duchy of Saxe-Meiningen, began to introduce his own ideas of how theatre ought to be produced. He began to supervise every component of every theatrical production created in his country and eventually developed a system of codification that directors have followed to varying degrees, ever since. He worked very closely with his third wife, former actress, Ellen Franz, and his stage manager and assistant director, Ludwig Chronegk, previously a Jewish comedian, and the changes made by this triumvirate were all-encompassing in magnitude.

One of his primary aesthetic ideas was that the "stage set be consistent with the stage space." Prior to the Duke's involvement, stock settings and box sets had been popular because they could be used repeatedly, therefore, settings did not show specific locations. Details on stage sets were nearly always done in paint, and three-dimensional units were almost never used. Under the Duke's direction, new scenery and properties were constructed for each show; he included the use of real doors, steps, tables and chairs. He incorporated the use of levels to break up the stage space and made sure that no set piece ever occupied center stage. He masked the proscenium arch with tree branches or other appropriate scenery and was extremely careful with how he positioned actors against painted scenery.

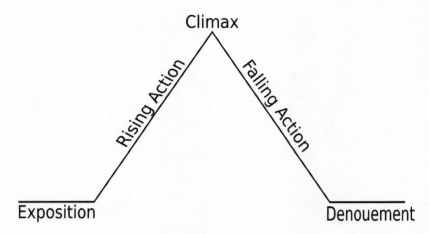

Freytags pyramid

In regard to the actors, instead of casting them according to their "lines of business" or particular character role they always played, i.e., ingénue, villain, rich older man, wicked city woman, etc., the actors were cast according to their talents and personalities. He would cast leading actors in small roles, lending gravitas to the smaller roles; he improved the level of acting in crowd scenes by having an experienced actor as a sort of acting coach in a group of extras.

Before the Duke began his campaign of reform, companies were assembled by gathering together actors who played specific character types. Once roles were assigned, it was the actor's responsibility to play that role on 24-hour notice. It was assumed that actors were competent and needed little help beyond establishing entrances and exits on stage. Blocking (the business of determining what characters move where and when and for what purpose) was not a priority; the stars took center stage, and everyone else stood in a line behind them.

Under the Duke's guidance, major changes occurred. Because his primary concern was the composition of the stage picture, he encouraged asymmetrical blocking; he objected to actors standing at center stage—he also discouraged parallel lines of actors. He liked staging realistic crowd scenes and was in fact famous for them. The scenery was constructed before rehearsals began, so the actors had the opportunity to work on the completed set from the beginning of the process. They also rehearsed with all of their performance props—the food and drink on stage were real. As the producer, as well as the director, the Duke controlled the finances, and because of this, rehearsals were able to continue until he thought the play was ready for an audience.

Meininger Theater II, Kramer, 2008

The most important innovation of Georg II, however, was influence of a solo perspective; his plays were produced with a specific vision or concept. The single-minded fervor demonstrated by the Duke toward his work in the theatre would probably be more closely aligned with how we currently regard an *auteur*, a term from film criticism that describes "a filmmaker whose individual style and complete control over all elements of production give a film its personal and unique stamp."

With modern directors, the role is much more a collaborative one. The Duke of Saxe-Meiningen took on all of the roles that are currently overseen by not only the director, but by designers, the dramaturge, publicity—in other words, a wide variety of people. Looking specifically at the role of the modern director, the first step is to choose a script. This may not be solely the director's choice; there may be others involved in the decision. Regardless, once the script is selected, the director begins to analyze it and to formulate a concept. There is no one way to do this—every director's method is unique to themselves.

For instance, some directors may want to consider the structure of the play. The text needs to have a clear *plot*, which is the arrangement of the events from the story. The playwright chooses particular elements from the story in order to present a specific perspective within the narrative. *Action* is required so that characters may be developed and delineated.

There must always be *conflict*, which is an opposition of forces. This opposition may be either character-based or situation-based, but either will give rise to the dramatic action. A facet that is essential to get things underway is the *inciting incident*. That is the event that starts the action moving.

It is necessary to have a balance of forces. The oppositional force tends to have its match within the play; characters need to have clear objectives which will drive them through the narrative and allow one side to eventually win out. That is often where you can hear the playwright's "voice" most clearly.

There are two basic structures in playwriting: *climactic* and *episodic*. In a climactic structure, all aspects of the play—duration, action and characters—are very tightly constructed. This type of structure is seen in Greek tragedy, where the plot begins very late in the story, near the climax. It covers a relatively short period of time, contains clearly defined scenes and tends to take place in a restricted locale. The narrative is linear, and the action proceeds in a cause-and-effect sequence.

An episodic structure follows a Brechtian Epic Theatre model, which you will read about in chapter 11. The plot begins fairly early in the story and moves through a series of episodes. It covers a longer period of time, sometimes months or even years. It is made up of numerous short, fragmented scenes and may change location frequently, ranging over cities or countries. There are many characters and often several parallel plot lines. Scenes tend to be juxtaposed to each other rather than follow in a cause-and-effect manner.

When the director begins to think about a concept or the overall vision of the play, there are a number of questions that can be asked. For instance, "When was it written?" "Were there certain social or cultural conditions that may have informed the writing? Is the play a period piece, or is it modern? If it is a period piece, can the production use a shift in period in order to highlight social, cultural, or political parallels? Is it appropriate to build a production around a central image or metaphor? It is essential to note that the concept should serve the play, rather than the other way around. As a director, you do not want the concept to overwhelm the playwright's voice.

When developing a concept, it is useful to find what director Harold Clurman (1901-1980) called the *spine* of the piece—what is the formulation of the action or conflict? To do this, you need to question the text in depth.

What is it about? Why are particular characters there? Why do they act as they do? What are their relationships to each other? This is an effective way for a director to understand the main action. There are potentially different spines for the same play.

> With *Hamlet*, for instance, several spines are possible: much will depend on the period in which the play is produced and on the point of view of the individual director. One spine could be simple revenge; another could be Hamlet's attempt to resolve his inner conflicts; still another could be Hamlet's attempt to locate and expose the duplicity and corruption he senses in Denmark. Clurman says that such varied interpretations are to be expected and are acceptable as long as the spine chosen remains true to the spirit and action of the play.

Another question to consider is what style will you be using, that is, in what manner will the play be presented? Is it realistic, nonrealistic, allegorical, or expressionistic? Depending upon the style you choose, there may be certain aspects that need specific attention. Time, for example, is fundamental in a play, yet it is problematic when trying to conceptualize it. Time is completely subjective; it takes a different shape for children than it does for adults, and it is valued differently by diverse cultures.

Then there are spatial elements. How is the space organized? What is the relationship between offstage action and what is happening onstage? What are the links between the space that is utilized and the fiction of the staged dramatic text?

The following is a well-known model for the acting areas of a proscenium stage. This is the point of view taken by all writers, actor and practitioners when working in the theatre:

You will notice that the area away from the audience is called the upstage area, closest to the audience is downstage. All of these positions are from the actors' perspective: imagine that you are the actor, standing on center stage, facing the audience. Center stage left would be your left, down stage right would be in front of you and to your right, up stage left would be behind you and to your left. This system does not vary; therefore, when a production's *prompt book* is examined, the notations can be read by anyone familiar with this model (the prompt book is the production script of the show that contains all of the information that would enable another company to recreate the performance from the very beginning of the process; it includes blocking, all lighting, sound and scenery cues, properties, contact information and so on).

"Many directors and designers conceive theatrical space, costumes, lighting and sound through healthy give-and-take and full collaboration." Generally speaking, directors and designers begin preliminary meetings before casting or rehearsals begin. Many times, the director will brainstorm ideas with the designers, presenting the ideas that s/he has had about the text, and receiving feedback from the design team, not only about the ideas themselves, but also about how well they will work when put into practice. The designers may take their inspirations from many sources but will work together with the director to create a unified production.

It requires numerous skills to become a successful director. There is the critical ability of being able to read and analyze a dramatic text; the director needs to be able to read people and understand how best to guide them in their own creative trajectory. It is extremely useful to be able to think and see in three dimensions, especially in discussions with designers. It is also a stressful and challenging career, since the director ultimately bears the responsibility for the success or failure of the production. There may be as many methods of directing as there are directors, but until the opening night of the play, when the director's job is finished, the director is at the center of all aspects of that production.

For Further Reading:

Francis Hodge. *Play Directing: Analysis, Communication and Style.* Boston: Allyn and Bacon, 2000.
Gabriella Giannachi and Mary Luckhurst, eds. *On Directing: Interviews with Directors.* New York: St Martin's Griffin, 1999.
Harold Clurman. *On Directing.* New York: Collier, 1972.
Lawrence Stern. *Stage Management.* Boston: Allyn and Bacon, 2000.

CHAPTER 5

WHO IS THE DESIGN TEAM?

Paul von Joukowsky-Bühnenbild Parsifal-Gralstempel, 1882

T HERE ARE THREE essential aspects that comprise the visual
design of any performance: set, costume, and lighting. These
design elements reflect the themes and mood, style, and emotions of a play,
as well as indicate the historical or geographic context of the production.
The design of a play is of fundamental importance to its conceptualization
by a director or, conversely, the director's initial conception of a play can
influence the design (or the designer) to work in a particular way. In both
cases, the design is open to another level of reception as it subsequently acts
as a communicator to the audience. The audience reception of the design
can be an important factor in a director's choice of the visual elements
of a production. Design is concerned with the way in which meaning

is developed and conveyed from the time a director first reads a play to the moment when the audience interprets it. Design elements need to be read together and incorporated into the bigger picture of theatrical space, audience layout, and acting style. A design properly conceived and executed should express the core meaning of the production. Set and costume designs are not just a collection of images; they are the representation of mood, the presence that enhances and comments on the performance. Design creates dramatic action, causes tension in a visual form; it is a signifier of performance meaning. Design is an integral part of the whole production process; it is disheartening to see designs, which lack coherence and are given a poor second place in any production.

This is not to say that any facet of design has to be elaborate or expensive. Some productions are staged without set or created environment, and this can be tremendously effective as long as there is strict unity between the design and other aspects of the production.

When a designer begins to work on a production, s/he starts in the same way as the director, e.g., by reading the play text. The designer and director Mordecai Gorelik (1899-1990) talked about finding the "dramatic metaphor," and suggested a series of questions in order to find it:

> What is the "atmosphere" of the locale? What quality does it have which makes it an integral part of this play and of no other play? What is the style of the author, what is notable about the historic period of the play or about its geographical location? What is the *dramatic metaphor* of each setting, and of the settings as a whole? What is the presumable history of the locale? What will the actors' movements be like? Will their actions around a table best convey the theme, or is a fireplace or stairway the natural center of the action?

There are two main approaches to creating a dramatic world onstage. The scenery may be representational; in other words, it may present a realistic view of the world, whether it is an interior or exterior set. If the scenery is presentation, then it is much less likely to resemble daily life. It is likely to be stylized or abstract or minimalist; whichever method has been chosen, the scenery is there as part of the overall *mise-en-scène* or visual theme of the production.

Rhinoceros.lw5

12/14/2011

William & Mary Theatre
Phi Beta Kappa Hall
February 24-27, 2011

directed by Laurie J. Wolf
scenery by Matthew Allar
lighting by Steve Holliday

Channel	Dim	Position	U#	Purpose	Color	Gobo	Instrument Type	Watt	Accessory
(1)	65	NO. 1 BEAM	16	DR BAX	L-116		PAR 64 ALT WFL	1kW	
(2)	61	NO. 1 BEAM	11	DC BAX	L-116		PAR 64 ALT WFL	1kW	
(3)	55	NO. 1 BEAM	5	DL BAX	L-116		PAR 64 ALT WFL	1kW	
(4)	87	NO. 1 ELECTRIC	15	R BAX	L-116		PAR 64 ALT WFL	1kW	
(5)	81	NO. 1 ELECTRIC	9	C BAX	L-116		PAR 64 ALT WFL	1kW	
(6)	76	NO. 1 ELECTRIC	4	L BAX	L-116		PAR 64 ALT WFL	1kW	
(7)	100	NO. 2 ELECTRIC	8	UR BAX	L-116		PAR 64 ALT WFL	1kW	
(8)	98	NO. 2 ELECTRIC	6	UC BAX	L-116		PAR 64 ALT WFL	1kW	
(9)	96	NO. 2 ELECTRIC	4	UL BAX	L-116		PAR 64 ALT WFL	1kW	
(11)	67	NO. 1 BEAM	18	DR BAX	N/C		S4 PAR WFL	750w	SCROLLER
(11.1)	269	NO. 1 BEAM	18.1	SCROLLER	SCROL L 2		FORERUNNER	100w	
(12)	63	NO. 1 BEAM	13	DC BAX	N/C		S4 PAR WFL	750w	SCROLLER
(12.1)	270	NO. 1 BEAM	13.1	SCROLLER	SCROL L 2		FORERUNNER	100w	
(13)	57	NO. 1 BEAM	7	DL BAX	N/C		S4 PAR WFL	750w	SCROLLER
(13.1)	266	NO. 1 BEAM	7.1	SCROLLER	SCROL L 2		FORERUNNER	100w	
(14)	88	NO. 1 ELECTRIC	16	R BAX	N/C		S4 PAR WFL	750w	SCROLLER
(14.1)	259	NO. 1 ELECTRIC	16.1	SCROLLER	SCROL L 2		FORERUNNER	100w	
(15)	83	NO. 1 ELECTRIC	11	C BAX	N/C		S4 PAR WFL	750w	SCROLLER
(15.1)	257	NO. 1 ELECTRIC	11.1	SCROLLER	SCROL L 2		FORERUNNER	100w	
(16)	77	NO. 1 ELECTRIC	5	L BAX	N/C		S4 PAR WFL	750w	SCROLLER

SCROLLS:

2.   R-00,R-58,R-39,L-201,R-65,R-68,R-80,R-71,L-116,R-08,L-147,R-21,R-337,L-127,R-26,L-156: R-00, R-58, R-39, L-201, R-65, R-68, R-80, R-71, L-116, R-08, L-147, R-21, R-337, L-127, R-26, L-156

Rhinoceros, Stephen Holiday, Department of Theater Speech and Dance,
College of William and Mary, 2011

The scenic designer also generally oversees the construction of the set properties. This includes furniture, both practical and decorative. There are times when the properties form the focus for the entire production, as in Eugene Ionesco's Absurdist piece, *The Chairs,* where two elderly characters pack the performance space with chairs that are never filled.

In order to see and augment what the scenic designer has put on stage, the lighting designer must visualize the type of lighting, which is to be used, its psychological effect, its color, and its intensity. The lighting design may be the most difficult aspect of design to communicate, because it is so ethereal; however, experienced designers are able to use sketches, computer images, colors and examples from nature to convey their ideas.

When s/he is analyzing the play, because the lighting designer, like everyone else, begins with reading the text, they will play close attention to the structure of the play, its mood and all possibilities for lighting. If it is a realistic or naturalistic piece, then the designer will not only want to illuminate the stage as realistically as possible, but will also want to use "practicals." A practical is a visible light source, such as a table lamp or perhaps the light from a television screen that is amplified with an additional light source. The light will come from the practical, but the additional instruments will boost the effect and intensify the light coming from the practical on the stage.

The lighting designer will create a lighting plot, which shows where the instrument is to be hung; this plot also indicates what type of instrument is to be used, as well as the filter color. Prior to technical rehearsals, the designer works with a lighting crew to hang, focus and filter the lighting instruments, and to set up the circuitry and the lighting console. During tech week, the lighting designer will write cues, i.e., indicating what combination of lights will go on or off at any particular point in the play and what intensity they should be. Many times this will change when the actors and their costumes are in a scene under the lights, but changes are generally minimal.

A lighting designer's position is a complicated one. S/he must have an in-depth understanding of the other design positions, must have a thorough comprehension of space and color, and must be able to paint and sculpt with light, a product that is the most ephemeral of all the design elements.

There are two major fields of study when it comes to designing costumes for the stage. The first is the study of life and character for people look the way they look because of the way they are. Each personal variation of dress springs from some variation of character or of mood, differences that may be slight but are nonetheless important. Had Hamlet been a well-adjusted and happy young prince, he would not have clung so tenaciously to his black garments.

The second area of study is the research into period and national costume. This encompasses not just the drawings and pictures in the costume books but includes all the paintings and applied arts and some of the writings of the period of research. Much available information about clothing and the social customs relating to it may be found in the writings of practically any time in recorded history.

Costumes work in synchronicity with the set and lighting to establish location and time frame of the play. Designers will usually share the information about the color palette they are intending to use so that all of the designers have the same information and can work in conjunction with one another. In addition to articulating concept and helping to establish the world of the play, costumes play an essential part in the audience's reception and appreciation for the characters on the stage. The costume designer must not only remember the needs of the character, but also the needs of the actor. Part of the actor's instrument is her/his body, and s/he needs to be able to work with and within the costume.

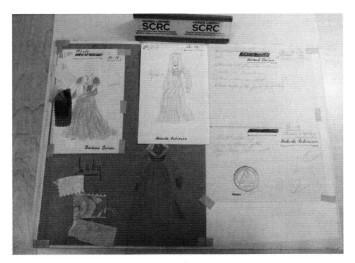

Two Ladies, Mordecai Gorelik, Gisela Cairobaza, 2012

The costume designer will usually show the director quick sketches that show basic ideas. When the director and designer come to an agreement, the designer will draw costume "renderings," and color pictures of the completed costumes on the actors. In addition, fabric swatches will be added to the rendering, so that the director or anyone looking at the renderings may see what fabrics will be used in the construction of the costumes.

Makeup design tends to go in and out of fashion as a design element. Often, the costume designer will take on this role, and the actors will apply their own makeup. For a realistic play, most young actors will need makeup that will emphasize the natural features of the face and to make them more distinctive under strong stage light. Makeup should be applied in strong light, but away from any glare. A good rule to remember is the smaller the theatre, the less make up is necessary.

There are currently several productions that utilize fantasy makeup. For instance, *The Lion King* requires its actors to apply makeup in imitation of various African animals. Fantasy makeup is fun to work with, but it needs to be planned, thought out in advance and practiced before it begins to look anything like a professional job.

Stage on Stage, Lekogm, 2004

The work of the sound designer is still one of the biggest variables in the theatre. Many theatre companies depend upon their lighting designer to take care of the sound design as well; however, sound design has been expanding and becoming a viable part of the design team. Many scripts call for sound effects or specific pieces of music, but that is just where the sound designer's job begins. Many directors are interested in a "soundscape" for their production. This is an ongoing recording of sounds that runs underneath the entire performance, always pertaining to what is happening in the production but, ideally, finding its way into the subconscious of the audience. For example, in a performance of Peter Weiss's *Marat/Sade*, a play set in a mental institution in 1808, the soundscape consisted of scraping sounds—keys turning in locks, clock's ticking, footsteps, water dripping, and the occasional scream, among other appropriate noises. This went on for the entire play, which lasted for one hour and forty minutes without an intermission. In a sense, a soundscape is an aural set design.

Sound designers are also responsible for adding music to plays where the director has decided to enhance the script for various reasons. The whole system of using microphones for a musical must be created and executed by a sound designer.

While not a design position, the role of the *dramaturge* is one that has received renewed interest in recent years. The European roots of production dramaturgy were codified and more clearly defined by the works of Denis Diderot (1713-1784) and Gotthold Lessing (1729-1781).

What exactly is a dramaturge and what does a dramaturge do? The *Oxford Encyclopaedia to Theatre and the Performing Arts* gives one of the best and most comprehensible definitions:

> A dramaturg is a person with a knowledge of the history, theory, and practice of theatre, who helps a director, designer, playwright or actor realise their intentions in a production. The dramaturg—sometimes called a literary manager, is an in-house artistic consultant cognizant of an institution's mission, a playwright's passion, or a director's vision, and who helps bring them all to life in a theatrically compelling manner. This goal can be accomplished in myriad ways and the dramaturg's role often shifts according to context and is always fluid. As there is no one way to create theatre, there is no single model of the dramaturg.

A dramaturge will read the script, attend rehearsals and production meetings and will do research for the company, based upon the director's concept and the designers' research. Frequently, the dramaturge will give a presentation to the company on the information found in the course of the research. As the *Oxford Encyclopaedia's* definition states, the role is "always fluid"; the nature of the dramaturge's working relationship with any production company may take any number of forms, depending on the play and the personalities involved.

And now to the stage manager, perhaps last in this chapter, but certainly never least in a production. The stage manager is the person who perhaps works most closely with the director throughout the entire production process. The stage manager is usually the busiest person in a production—organizing, creating timetables, solving problems and making sure that everything is running according to schedule. The best stage managers handle the day-to-day issues (late actors, rehearsal discipline, paperwork) so that the director can concentrate on the artistic concerns of the performance.

The stage manager is also responsible for the promptbook, referred to in chapter 4. This is the copy of the script that contains all the cuts, blocking (movement of the actors), stage business and all cues—lighting, sound, set and costume changes.

During the final week of rehearsals, the stage manager begins to take over the technical side of the show by organizing the different technical crews, calling cues and running the rehearsal under show conditions. Once the show opens, the director's job ends, and the stage manager takes over. In the professional theatre, it is not unusual for a stage manager to take on the responsibilities of rehearsing understudies or new cast members in the director's absence.

In addition to having exceptional organizational skills, a stage manager must be an outstanding people person. The relationship between the director and stage manager is essential for a smooth running production, and the stage manager must be able to communicate directly and well with the design team and the technicians. In addition, s/he must be extremely diplomatic when dealing with actors. Discipline must be maintained at all times but not at the expense of the company morale.

As we can see, collaboration is requisite when it comes to directing and designing a production. Not only is it nearly impossible for one design area to work in isolation from the others, it just does not make any sense for that to happen. Theatre is a collaborative art and all those involved—actors, directors, designers, technicians and audience members—all have a role to play.

Play for Study: Eugene Ionesco's Rhinoceros

Although Ionesco freely admitted that the expansion of the Nazi party during the 1930's in Germany was a specific incitement for *Rhinoceros*, he by no means restricted the thematic content of the play to a condemnation of Nazism alone. Instead, he used the growth of this movement as an archetype of ideologies in general, and he used it to expound on the essentially dehumanizing effect of all ideological movements.

Ionesco made a point of stating that his artistic purpose in *Rhinoceros* was farther reaching than merely education: "*Rhinoceros* is, to be sure, an anti-Nazi work, but it is above all also a work directed against all collective hysteria and the epidemics which assume the guise of reason, but which are nevertheless serious maladies for which ideologies are no more than alibis. If you perceive that history has lost its sense of reason, that the facts and the ideologies that propagate them, if you take a clear look at reality, that will be enough to deter you from succumbing to irrational 'reasons' and to escape the delirium."

Rhinoceros is considered to be an example of Theatre of the Absurd, and it clearly follows the guidelines as set out in chapter 10: "Out of harmony with reason or propriety; incongruous, unreasonable, illogical" (Ionesco). It also has elements of Existential angst. Berenger's stand against the rhinos reflects how he stands alone against the social order and can "only act" or use his freedom. The alienated and isolated nature of human beings with only the agony of choice to accompany them is something that we see Berenger embodies when his whole world turns against him, and he is the only human being left. In his resistance as being "the last man," he has only his freedom, and this is ultimately what turns Berenger an existentialist hero.

For Further Reading:

Arnold Aronson. *American Set Design*. New York: Theatre Communications Group, 1985.

Douglas A Russell. *Costume History and Style*. Boston: Allyn and Bacon, 1983.

Howard Bay. *Stage Design*. New York: Drama Book Specialists, 1974.

Lynn Pecktal. *Costume Design: Techniques of Modern Masters*. New York: BackStage Books, 1999.

Richard Pilbrow. *Stage Lighting Design*. London: Nick Hern Books, 1997.

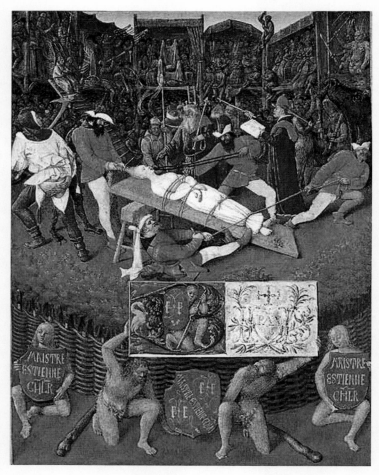

Sainte Apolline, Jean Fouquet, 15th Century

CHAPTER 6

MEDIEVAL AND ENGLISH RENAISSANCE THEATRE

Waites-in-York, Benyon, 2010

WE HAVE BEEN examining the roles of the audience, actor, director, and designers fairly closely and some of the preparatory work that must go into the development of their respective crafts. As noted, the focus of theatre is people—how they react to one another, what their place is in society, and how the various aspects, both behind and in front of the curtain, come together to create a unique piece of theatre. It is also important to consider what might be appropriate and appealing. In order to address this side of the theatre, we will be looking at the characteristics of Medieval and Renaissance theatre, focusing primarily on English-based drama.

European society during the Middle Ages consisted of three primary groups: peasants who tilled the soil, secular lords, and ecclesiastical lords. The Church provided the principal outlets for artistic expression; organized theatrical activities had virtually disappeared in Western Europe. The surviving theatrical elements included remnants of the Roman mimes, popular festivals, pagan rites, and Christian ceremonies.

It is useful to begin with a short history of the development of medieval theatre. Often set aside as naïve and unoriginal, medieval theatre on the European continent kept alive the natural human desire to act, to mimic, and to experience vicariously what could not be known in a given life. Early medieval church services contained rituals that were very similar to our modern conception of drama. The earliest "dramatic" piece was the *Quem quaeritis* trope (c.925):

> Scholarly opinion has come to differ widely about specific way the *Quem quaeritis* trope developed into medieval mysteries. According to some reconstructions of the most elaborate form of this proto-drama, two choirs, usually situated on opposite sides of the nave or cross-bar of the cathedral, or on opposite sides of the church doors, address each other with the first two and second two lines of this short paraphrase from the Vulgate Bible. The "three Marys" come to his tomb on the third day after his crucifixion only to find the stone rolled away from its door and an angel standing in the doorway. The angel asks them the question in the first line, they reply with the second line, and the angel answers their request with the last two lines:

> > Whom seek ye in the sepulchre, O Christians?
> > Jesus of Nazareth, who was crucified, O angel.
> > He is not here, He has arisen as He foretold:
> > Go, announce that He has arisen from the grave.

By the tenth century these church services and tropes had become short plays, which were mimed and chanted by monks and choirboys. By the thirteenth century, the plays had become much more elaborate and also very popular. Comedy was gradually introduced into the stories, which precluded them from inclusion in church services. Consequently, the church authorities decided to transfer the plays to the church grounds, just about the time the clergy stopped taking part in the plays.

The organization of the plays was taken over by the trade "guilds" (associations of tradesmen in particular trades), and sequences of plays known as *Mystery Cycles* were created. Each guild acted a play suited to its profession, and the play was performed on a mobile *pageant wagon* at several different locations around the town. After each performance, the wagon was moved to its next location, and the play was repeated. By remaining in one position, an audience would see the Bible story enacted in its entirety, each scene being performed on a different cart by a different guild.

In most towns, the mystery plays were performed on the feast of Corpus Christi (the Thursday after Trinity Sunday), with the exception of the Chester cycle, which was performed during Whitsun week (beginning the seventh Sunday after Easter).

There are only few copies of the cycle plays remaining to us today. Because few members of the medieval guild could read, there was little point in making numerous copies of scripts. However, there are extant copies of the plays that were performed in York (forty-eight plays), Chester (twenty-four plays) and Wakefield (thirty-two plays). Several of the plays performed at Coventry have also survived.

Christmas and Easter themes represent the greatest number of liturgical plays. Other New Testament themes included the Raising of Lazarus, the Conversion of Saint Paul and plays about the Blessed Virgin. Highly developed plays about Lazarus are found in the Benediktbeuern Passion Play and in the Fleury playbook. The plays about the Blessed Virgin, destined to attain great popularity in the vernacular miracle plays, followed scriptural or apocryphal texts in the liturgical drama. The four most important feasts celebrated the Presentation on November 21, the Annunciation on March 25, the Purification on February 2 and the Assumption on August 15.

The medieval psyche took an unsophisticated and direct approach to life; their belief was that the universe was finite, that God created and ended it. It was for that reason that all of the mystery cycles began with God on his throne, stating:

Ego sum alpha et omega,
I am the first, the last also,
One god in majesty . . .

In this way, the cycle plays demonstrated the idea that all past and all future were in the present. There is a standard practice in the following ten plays that appears in various forms in each cycle: (1) Fall of Lucifer, (2) Creation of Man, (3) Cain and Abel, (4) Noah and the Flood, (5) Abraham and Isaac, (6) Birth of Christ, (7) Raising of Lazarus, (8) Passion of Christ, (9) Resurrection, and (10) Last Judgment. There is a clear pattern to these particular plays appearing in each cycle: each is divided into three main sections. The first section is the Creation, which brings about the fall of Mankind and necessitates the second coming of God. This leads to the second section, which follows the life of Christ as a redeemer. The final section focuses on the final judgment of the human race, where the second coming of God provides a moral choice.

In contrast to the medieval plays, where drama largely evolved from the rites commemorating birth and the resurrection of Christ, during the Renaissance, we can see the beginning of drama as we now know it—an image of human life revealed in successive events and told in dialogue and action for the entertainment and instruction of an audience.

The Renaissance means many things about an amorphous period in political, economic, scientific and above all, cultural history, involving a number of Western countries at various stages in their development. The scholarly attempts to block it off with dates, however generally assigned, confuse more than they clarify because the phenomenon made itself felt at different times in different places. The single fact of which one can be sure is that it all began in Italy, sometime in the fourteenth century and then later spread to other parts of Europe.

Renaissance or rebirth has to do with a spirit of self-rediscovery whereby human beings engaged in an exercise of mind and body, viewing themselves as creatures of this world as they did in antiquity (hence the pagan presence juxtaposed with Christian belief). It was this process of self-discovery that made possible outer discovery, e.g., Copernicus or Galileo. The renaissance produced a confident state of essence that made humans the measure of all things, with their own reason for being.

Although science acquired fresh vitality in this atmosphere, it was the arts that really symbolized new life for modern civilization. The rediscovery stemmed in large part from an aesthetic view of the self and humanism, absorbing and refashioning the intellectual visions of ancient Greece and Rome and kindling a new desire for learning for its own sake. It was natural for drama and theatre, then, to make full use of the humanized language and prolific motivation that was infecting the greater part of Europe.

Although Italy (like France until its Age Classique) cannot boast of the copious and genial drama that characterized Elizabethan England and the Spanish Golden Age, Italian influence shaped dramatic production all over Europe, not only by virtue of its humanistic spirit derived from the classical tradition, but also by virtue of how it developed the actor's craft by training performers in mime, voice, acrobatics, choreography, and other essentials. In France, popular theatre, as in the case of the *parades*, remained outdoors in squares and fairs on improvised stages for some time, serving as a crowd grabber for hucksters selling their potions and remedies. Initially, actors were plebeian performers with no particular training. Only toward the end of the sixteenth century did professional groups form—troupes that moved indoor, taking account of Italian innovations. In time, some groups acquired high visibility, such as the Théâtre du Marais and Moliere's Illustre Théâtre. Paris had only one theatre—the Hôtel de Bourgogne in the early seventeenth century—when London had six.

Hôtel de Bourgogne, Gravure d' Abraham Bosse, 1634

A similar evolution, again heavily Italianate, may be traced in Spain during the sixteenth and seventeenth centuries, except that there was a broader segment of the public that concerned itself closely with theatre. This meant that standards of performance as well as behavior were also based on the Italian model, despite the author and playwright Miguel de Cervantes's efforts to remove drama from the plebs and give it a more sophisticated, classical setting. Actors tended to be adventurers (for example, the "Carro de la muerte" as *Don Quixote de la Mancha*), often of questionable ethics, who pilfered what they could if gate receipts got low. Roving companies performed on platforms, erected for the occasion with rickety supports, in courtyards called *corrales* or out on the squares. Two coarse wooden theatres existed in Madrid shortly thereafter, the Corral de la Cruz and the Corral del Príncipe.

Across the Channel, when the Tudors (1485-1603) opened England to the splendors of the Renaissance, Italian books and scholars gained great popularity at the court of Queen Elizabeth I. Under her father, Henry VIII, the theatre was looked down on (part of his Decree of 1531 labels actors "vagabonds") because of the unsavory character of many of its practitioners, but in the new atmosphere, actors managed to take advantage of the prevailing interest in drama and seek the protection of court lords, indeed also of sovereigns. Not even the Puritan clergy could prevail. Previously outlawed, strolling players became respectable, enjoying legal protection together with other benefits. King Richard III, Henry VIII (his decree notwithstanding) and Elizabeth I, through Lord Leicester (Robert Dudley, who was more interested in players than was the queen), kept companies, some of which might actually go on tour.

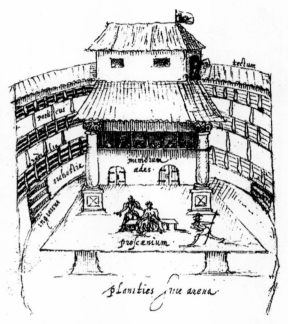

The Swan, Johannes de Witt, 1596

Like Molière, Shakespeare also acted until 1603. Many other companies like guilds, became "recognized," and a 1572 law, making the recognition exclusive by "privilege," encouraged James Burbage four years later to establish the first public theatre at Shoreditch, The Theatre, built in a circular shape of timber. A white flag flown aloft indicated comedy, a black one, tragedy. Also round and unroofed was The Curtain (London, 1577), and this was followed a decade later by Philip Henslowe's The Rose, then The Fortune (Finsbury, 1600), and The Hope (1613), the last unroofed London playhouse. After 1620, all playhouses were roofed. With companies flourishing in them, the theatres increased in number from eight to twenty between 1600 and 1616, when Shakespeare died. Theatrical activities took place everywhere, from private homes and public squares to universities. The upper class sat separately from the others, either in lower balconies (the gallery remained for the commoners) or, when French habits encroached, directly onstage. All in all, though the actors had to shout their lines (Hamlet inveighed against the performer who would "split the ears of the groundling [and] out-herod Herod"), English enthusiasm for the theatre made the event not as quarrelsome as it tended to be in France or Spain. Still, Hamlet could wish for a calm, cultured audience over a low public. From the pit, the "groundlings" would shout their approval or lack of it, regardless of whether the majority of spectators thought differently. No doubt the actors raised their voices to compete, and the open roof did not help matters acoustically. Accordingly, gestures became broader and more expressive—a positive result of the conditions, along with greater clarity of diction. Another positive development was the "spoken decor," the stylistic feature whereby the scenery was explained in the play's text.

A Master of the Revels for Elizabeth's private theatre, such as Edmund Tilney, who during his tenure, from 1579 to 1610, could censor all public stages (the practice did not cease until 1968). Yet the bulk of the performances took place in public structures, and here, too, the enthusiasm of the acting companies inspired very innovative performances, which may be credited with having stimulated the three-dimensionality of Shakespearean characters as contrasted with the bland two-dimensionality of so many Italian Renaissance characters. Although historical consciousness was not such then as to prescribe chronological accuracy for costumes, the Elizabethan stage indulged itself lavishly in opulent garments, and this condition affected others. The English adopted the medieval concept of a multiple stage and combined it with that of the thrust stage, whereby the proscenium protrudes into the audience. The whole effect was a veritable spectacle, complete with musical interludes, or even improvisations by a clown or buffoon (to Shakespeare's displeasure), but the overall experience was wholesome and substantial and brought forth actors of true stature—Edward Alleyn for Christopher Marlowe and Richard Burbage for Shakespeare.

Play for Study: Christopher Marlowe's Doctor Faustus

The Tragicall Historie of Doctor John Faustus is often viewed as a transition between Medieval and Renaissance thinking as it relates to drama and theatre. It is seen as a play with strong elements of both periods—stylistically as well as ideologically. *Doctor Faustus* has been described as a morality play, that is, a struggle between good and evil. What is missing from the play, however, is the idea of salvation as a beautiful concept (in Medieval Christian terms). Faustus sees Christianity as a limitation on his aspirations and interprets it as a control over his choices.

Faustus-Tragedy, John Wright, 1620

Marlowe is very careful throughout the course of the play to show both the Medieval and Renaissance view of Heaven and Hell. We are exposed to both the physical manifestations of hell (devils, demons, Lucifer, Mephistopheles), as well as the metaphysical side of Heaven, demonstrated by the debates between Doctor Faustus and Mephistopheles regarding the relationship between God and Man as a state of mind.

The play is divided into three major sections or issues. The first is Faustus's choice of damnation. We see him at the beginning of the play, reviewing his achievements. He realizes that although he has reached the pinnacle in the fields of logic, medicine, law and necromancy, he is still Faustus and "just a man." What he wants, of course, is to be a god. Instead, he goes to God's opposite and offers his soul. What he does not understand is that he has not left the sphere of Christianity.

The second section takes place in Act IV. This is when the realization dawns that what he has sold his soul for is valueless. His disillusion grows with his actions; he begins to use his powers in trivial ways because he, himself, has become trivial.

The last section takes place during the final act, when Faustus is alone in his study and pleads for mercy (which is not given), but never repents. He refuses to reject his humanist aspirations and retains his independence; however, he is forever damned for this and at the end of the scene is dragged into the mouth of hell and torn apart.

Marlowe presents both sides to the argument of humanist thinking; that is the reason it is said the play embodies both Medieval and Renaissance doctrines. The play does not preach pious submission to blind law; however it is a pessimistic statement on independent thinking and free choice. We are not always clear exactly what Marlowe is questioning or what he is condemning—or if he is.

As we have seen, people and beliefs were widely diverse, from the time of the Middle Ages to the Renaissance. Even this is a partially inaccurate statement because these time frames covered centuries; therefore, it would have been impossible for modes and trends to remain static throughout. We have looked at some of the more representative types of drama and theatre during these eras and will examine the Restoration in the next chapter.

For Further Reading:

Gerald E Bentley. *The Professions of Dramatist and Player in Shakespeare's Time, 1590-1642.* Princeton, NJ: Princeton University Press, 1984.

J R Mulryne and Margaret Shewring. *Theatre of the English and Italian Renaissance.* New York: St Martin's, 1991.

Richard Beadle. *The Cambridge Guide to Medieval Theatre.* Cambridge: Cambridge University Press. 1994.

Ronald Vince. *Ancient and Medieval Theatre.* Westport, Conn.: Greenwood, 1984.

CHAPTER 7

ITALIAN RENAISSANCE THEATRE

T HEATRICAL ARCHITECTURE FOUND its revival during the Renaissance. The architectural style was typical of the revivalist age, dominated by ancient art forms and integrated with modern ideas. Though in the Renaissance interpretation, contributions from Filippo Brunelleschi (1377-1446), Leon Batista Alberti (1404-1472), Leonardo da Vinci (1452-1519), Michelangelo (1475-1574), and Bramante (1444-1514) cannot be ignored, it was the works of Palladio (1508-1580), Serlio (1475-1554), and Furttenbach (1591-1667) that can be termed as evolutionary in this genre. Not only did these leaders form and start modern art ornaments like decorative designing and mechanical effects, but they were also responsible for establishing of principles of theatrical architecture.

Teatro Olimpico, 1908

Today English and Italian theatres still resonate with the creations of the past. What made the role of theatres most significant was the fact that audiences were presented with plays in a proscenium format. The background of the plays, the effects as well as the sound, played an important role in enhancing the storyline. In the Renaissance, while period plays acted as a medium for transference of culture and social messages, the theatres acted as a tool for enhancing the meaning. In this manner, Renaissance theatres proved important tools for transferring contemporary culture to the public of today.

Italian theatres were considered as a revival of European theatres. These were based on the recreational nature of the theatres known as the neoclassicist movement. The Renaissance interpretation of ancient theatre designs therefore became the epitome for theatrical arts in Italy.

Carolus Borromeus interior, Ad Meskens, 1521

Commedia dell'Arte began during the Italian Renaissance or at least came to notice then. Its origins are disputed, with some authorities tracing its origins back to Roman times, and insisting that the style began in the fourteenth century. By the sixteenth century, the art form developed into a popular performing style in Italy and spread from there throughout Europe. Commedia dell'Arte remained popular for approximately two hundred years but never really died out and still exists today. The term itself is difficult to define. Generally, it means "comedy of the professional players." A Commedia refers to a drama that employs comedy and has a happy ending. Commedia dell'Arte involved improvised performances of a previously selected subject. In short, the actors knew the plot but made up the dialogue and actions during the course of the performance. This allowed actors to develop humorous scenarios on the spot that had nothing to do with the ostensible scenario. Typically, subjects included adultery, love, old age and jealousy. Bawdy topics were particularly popular, and situations were often developed that led to one of the female characters disrobing. The comedic improvised activities might include such things as acrobatics, juggling, wrestling or anything that the actors could think of, including humorous repartee with each other. One famous improvised stunt involved a character doing a somersault while holding a glass of wine and not spilling a drop. Improvised dialogue had to be humorous and well-timed. These comedic interludes were called lazzi. Actors often tried to incorporate local occurrences and topics into the play. An actor often played the same character for his or her entire performing career, allowing him or her to become very proficient in his or her performance. People often came to see the added comedy in performances instead of the main story. Plots usually revolved around a pair of young, attractive lovers (Innamorato and Innamorata) and a cast of other characters. The play was divided into acts with a prologue and scenes. When the prescribed scenario was filled in, actors could embellish and enhance their parts. Both men and women performed in the plays. Prior to Commedia, all parts in theatre were usually played by males. This changed with the Commedia tradition. There were even some troupes who were led by women (e.g., the Gelosi company, under the direction of Isabella Andreini). There was a convention that certain characters always appeared with masks or half masks. The lovers, however, never wore masks.

Harlequin and Antoinette, Bouffonz, 2010

Some of the stock characters who appeared in every play were Pantalone, a rich, old miser, the Doctor, a long-winded lawyer, philosopher or astrologer, the Captain, a flamboyant braggart who is a coward at heart and Arlecchino (Harlequin), an acrobat clown or valet. Arlecchino carried a large baton called a "slapstick" that he used to hit the other characters, leading to today's slapstick comedy. Generally, the stock characters were divided into three groups, the lovers, the Vecchi or old men, who try to keep the lovers apart, and the Zanni, clownish servants, who distracted the Vecchi from their goal. Much of the humor came from the Zanni characters and our word "zany" is derived from the term. Over time, each set of characters developed certain characteristics, making it possible for the audience to anticipate the attitudes and actions of the characters.

Commedia dell'Arte made many contributions to modern comedy. First, timing was important in the repartee and has been in comedy ever since. Second, slapstick comedy, such as that practiced by Chaplin, Keaton, and Lloyd, is a direct descendent of Commedia dell'Arte. Third, modern romantic comedy had its origins in the plots and characters of Commedia dell'Arte. Finally, both situation comedy and animated cartoons employ elements of Commedia dell'Arte.

One of the contributions of Commedia dell'Arte to Western theatre, in addition to those mentioned above, was the emergence of acting as a profession. Previously, there had been professional performers, but they did not specialize in acting. During the Middles Ages, most theatrical performances were morality plays with many of them based on the Bible. Church authorities frowned on any other type of acting. But the timing, skill and professionalism demanded by Commedia dell'Arte forced performers to become full-time actors. This concept spread across Western Europe, including England. Once acting became a full-time profession, the techniques of acting began to develop, as the better performers began to hone their craft and pass on their knowledge to new actors. The stock characters of Commedia dell'Arte also led to the modern character actor, who specializes in playing certain parts. These characters clearly influenced Shakespeare and Moliere. This sort of specialization had never been seen before in the Western world during the Middle Ages and ancient times. Troupes of traveling professional actors were formed as well, usually with a nobleman as a patron.

One of the most prominent features of the Renaissance theatres was the emergence of court theatres. The name stems from the manner in which they were created. The court theatres came into existence through the conversion of tennis courts. During the eighteenth century, most of the elites were fond of tennis; many rich families had tennis courts to entertain their guests. But by the end of the century, this trend diminished significantly. To make use of their space, the families converted their tennis courts to open-air theatres. These became so popular that gradually it was the only accepted form of theatrical performance. One of the reasons for the popularity was the changing society. People were developing different preferences and tastes and had developed great affinity toward musical shows, particularly the *principesche* court. This was a sort of tennis court built like the structure of a palace to give the illusion of rich living quarters. The *teatro* were equipped with exclusive services and were designed in horseshoe shapes that one can still see dominate in today's theatrical construction. The Teatro Olimpico was one of the most prominent, modeled in Roman style. This style usually consisted of multiple doorways with unique perspectives from every door with the auditorium in a horseshoe shape.

The Teatro Olimpico has its origin from Palladio and was designed for Vicenza Accademia Olimpica to stage his performances. This model was a suggestion of the classical theatre design of the Greeks. It was also one of the surviving theatres from the Renaissance period. The theatre was constructed with an exterior brick box, using wooden interiors in semicircles of steep tiers for seating. The seat bench was carved out of wood facing the rectangular "proscenium stage." According to a description by Great Building Online, the interior has

> a wooden colonnade with cornice and figures above circle the top of the seats. The ceiling plane is undifferentiated and was later painted blue, suggesting an open sky above the theatre. The walls and ceiling of the proscenium are elaborately articulated with architectural details and statues, made of wood and plaster. A central arched opening dominates the back wall, flanked by two smaller doorways. Through these openings, elaborate stage sets of streets angle backstage, a triad through the central opening and single streets through each side. These sets, designed later by Scamozzi, use techniques of tilting the floors and contracting the angle between the street walls and the heights of their building facades to make foreshortened streets in perspective.

One can thus see why the theatres are still recognized as brilliant work in modern art, worked intricately on architectural principles.

Another designer, Sebastiano Serlio, whose architectural design were based on classical ideas and perspective of "periaktoi" (three-dimensional, triangular set pieces) created models which were used for setting up stages for plays that emphasized the realistic illusion for tragedies, for comedy, street scenes and for satyr plays, the countryside. The elements of portrayal pertained to external features rather than internal, because these stages were meant to recreate Roman scenarios from Greek plays. Other designers followed his trend to create *teatro all'antico* in 1589, which emphasized on the creation of solid backdrop and huge stage arches. But it was the decorative props introduced in 1618 by Giovanni Battista Aleotti and later on by Giacomo Torelli that really changed the face of stage decorations. Nicolo Sabattini and Leone de Sommi first introduced the shift in designs from presentation to mechanical handling of the props. They introduced lighting such as footlights, techniques for colored lights as well as dimming lights. These additions to staging became the epitome of development from classical to the neoclassical conception of theatrical designs.

Perspective scene design by Sabbattini, 1638

The purpose of theatre at the time was to entertain the rich. The designers based their plans on providing the effects for the benefit of the audience.

Since, the Italians were undergoing a revolution, art became the focus of their conceptualization. One of the main concepts was to create realistic art form. As a result, theatres became their obsession, a medium through which they could depict reality, as they envisioned it. The architects and designers of this period concentrated on providing a realistic background and real staging to the audience in order to tantalize their imagination. They were so focused on this goal that they even included in their designs the baroque style scenes of gardens, the fussy details of sculptures through intricate woodwork and the real-life-like lighting effects to differentiate day and night. The Renaissance was basically more influential on the English but the Italians were the main perpetrators. It was a period of restoration and recreation. Theatres no longer remained in the domain of the courts only and the common people were also able to enjoy this privilege.

From Greek theatres, the elements of development could be seen quite clearly. There was a shift of dramatic principles from exposure to enclosure. The focus of the designs gradually changed from a multiple eye focus point to variant focus. The illusionists could now design complicated situations for the scenes on the floor as well as the wings to depict scenes of the heavens. The use of shutters and vanishing points played important roles in providing dynamic stages for the actors to effectively play out their roles.

In this race for revolutionary theatre creation, Serlio took the lead. He proposed a broad perspective of the background through the use of paintings, scenic views and taking the illusion of real life scenes to depict the internal staging. His works corresponded with tragedy, comedy and satirical theatrical works. These plays required painted backdrops, three pairs of angled side wings and freestanding units to cover the space on either side of the stage. What was unique about Serlio's scenes was the fact that they were permanent. But the producers could manipulate them according to the needs of the performance.

Serlio was also responsible for introducing one of the first practical staging systems in 1600 when a flat wing and groove system, consisting of flat canvas covered frames with different scenes painted on them were staged on the floor. These could be pulled offstage, with another scene behind it. Although Serlio's ideas were not perfect, they were nevertheless evolutionary in the field of theatrical art forms.

With the help of Palladio and Serlio, Italian theatre staging like those illustrated in Virtuvius's *De Architectura* (1486) and *Dell'Architettura* (1545) set the paradigm for theatre designs. What these innovators did was reconstruct the theory of outdoor circular theatre works and convert them to indoor styles. They provided a new perspective to theatre creations. Although the only Renaissance Theatre still in existence is the Teatro Olimpico in Vicenza, Italy, other theatres like Teatro Farnes in Parma are remembered for their permanent proscenium arch and the illusion of perspective.

The single point perspective characterized Italian staging during the sixteenth, seventeenth and eighteenth centuries. This provided a more comprehensive background for the actors. Furthermore, the division of the raked stage between the upstage and downstage areas was created to provide a sense of depth to the scenario.

The semicircle auditoriums were typical characteristics of these theatres. The architects designed them with the sole aim of placing the elite at the top so that they would have a better view and to be able to move about to socialize, while the middle and lower class sections of the audience had permanent or no seating. Even in theatrical designs, one could see that the boxes were indicators of social classification. Hence, the designs of the Renaissance gave insights to the class system of the time.

Instrumental to the Renaissance theatres were the use of candles and oil lamps. The chandeliers were the main attraction, but it was the use of candles behind the proscenium arch and the footlights behind wings that gave Italian theatres the status they held in Europe. Even at that time, the use of dimmers was pervasive and was included to create shifts of sceneries and to make them more dramatic.

During the Renaissance, the element of realism was important for the audience to feel the totality of the play's concept. In today's theatres, lighting and effects are no longer a treat but a compulsion. Many theatres cannot be dynamic unless they are fully equipped with a lighting system, sound effects, and some sort of stage scenery change mechanism. That is why the theatrical contributors of the Italian Renaissance were considered great forward thinkers in their fields. What we take for granted, we owe to these artists and designers.

For Further Reading:

David Brubaker. *Court and commedia: The Italian Renaissance stage.* n.p.: R Rosen Press, 1975.
Michele Marrapodi. *Italian Culture in the Drama of Shakespeare & His Contemporaries.* New York: Ashgate Publishing Company, 2007.

Peter Murray. *The Architecture of the Italian Renaissance*. New York: Schocken, 1997.

Ronald W. Vince. *Neoclassical Theatre: A Historiographical Handbook*. New York: Greenwood, 1988.

LAURIE J. WOLF

CHAPTER 8

RESTORATION, NEOCLASSICISM, AND EIGHTEENTH-CENTURY ENGLISH THEATRE

Thomas Betterton as Hamlet, Nicholas Rowe, 1709

T HE PERIOD OF time in English history following the accession of Charles II to the throne is commonly referred to as the Restoration. Following the death of Elizabeth I, James I (James VI of Scotland) succeeded to the British throne. During his reign there was an ongoing political struggle over the control of church and state. The people were less concerned about the monarchy than they were about the money they paid toward taxes. Because the House of Commons attempted to use its control of the country's financial resources to control the state, "the Stuart monarchy began to use against the Parliamentary opposition those instruments of repression formerly directed against feudal separatism and peasant revolt. James I elaborated his theory of divine right of kings in response to opposition theories of the superiority of Parliament . . . The whole machinery of the state was bent to serve the purposes of royal policy."

At the same time, England was undergoing a struggle over control of the Church. The church courts were part of the state administrative machine: "Any independent thinker was likely to oppose a persecuting church whose leading officials were enforcing an unpopular government policy by supernatural sanctions. In the early seventeenth-century two worlds were at war: the whole power of Catholic Europe was aligned against the new forces fighting for the right of self-expression."

This questioning of the authority of church and state led to the first revolution in British history (1641), a civil war (1642), the execution of Charles I (James's son) (1649) and the restoration of Charles II in 1660. These radical actions resulted in a dramatic change among the citizens of the country. "The principle of individual conscience gave birth to innumerable dissenting groups within the Puritan movement . . . [Various] religious sects . . . proposed revolutionary concepts of liberty."

Nell Gwyn, Peter Lely, circa 1675

LAURIE J. WOLF

Charles II spent much of his time in Europe travelling to different countries (he resided in the Spanish Netherlands for four years, for instance, making him an attractive ally to Spain following his restoration to the throne) and viewing all forms of entertainment; he was especially impressed with the theatres. When he returned to England and restored his throne in 1660, he made a number of proclamations that had a direct impact on how the theatres were to be operated—proclamations that differed greatly from traditional methods. Historically and legally, women were not allowed to appear onstage. This convention went as far back as the ancient Greeks and with the possible exception of medieval actors, this was a convention that continued until the seventeenth century. One of the first edicts handed down by the new king was that women only were to play women's parts, and by mid-1661 onward, actresses had become an established feature of the Restoration stage. This convention became law in 1662.

The king also awarded patents to two theatre companies, King's Company and Duke of York's Men, under the direction of two middle-aged playwrights, Thomas Killegrew and William Davenant, respectively. Both Killegrew and Davenant produced works by new playwrights as well as adaptations of Renaissance plays. The Restoration playwrights became extremely popular with their comedies of manner and intrigue, in particular Sir George Etherege (*The Man of Mode*), William Wycherley (*The Country Wife*), William Congreve (*The Way of the World*) and George Farquhar (*The Recruiting Officer*). Also at this time was the appearance on the scene of the first professional female playwright, Aphra Behn (1640-1689), whose play *The Rover* will be discussed later in this chapter.

The characteristics of Restoration comedy were relatively simple, although the themes of the plays were anything but straightforward. Also known as Comedy of Manners due to the fact that they were centered on the aristocracy and landed gentry, they generally focused on the themes of love, sexual intrigue and cuckoldry. They were noted for their wit and clever word play and were set in the London parks, coffee houses and homes of the well-to-do. The character types included the dashing rake, the deceived older husband, the young, faithless wife and possibly a charismatic young heroine, who may or may not end up with the rake.

Restoration tragedy, by contrast, was a rather poor affair. There were very few Restoration playwrights writing new tragedies: John Dryden and Thomas Otway were the two notable exceptions. Most of the other tragedies that were being produced were adaptations of classical tragedies, including those by Shakespeare and other Renaissance playwrights. One of the main and most obvious problem with the adaptations was the way in which the playwrights tinkered with the original. Although not a tragedy, Shakespeare's *The Tempest*, as reworked by William Davenant and John Dryden, gives Miranda a sister, Dorinda; Caliban also gets a sister, Sycorax, named for their mother; Prospero has a foster son, Hippolito, who has never set eyes on a woman. This last character was a well-known *breeches* part, a phenomenon of the Restoration theatre where a female actor would don male garb (that would deliberately enhance her physical attributes) and play the role of a young man. *The Tempest or The Enchanted Island* was one of the most popular adaptations during the Restoration.

While this was going on in England, Molière's greatest comedies and Racine's greatest tragedies were being written and performed in France. "In Molière's view it would seem that the most disastrous of human error, errors we might wish to call tragic, might be envisaged by the mind as comic. That this view of things often induces or sparks off laughter, no sane person would deny." Molière was a writer who excelled in character studies; he enjoyed stripping away the social masks of people in any sort of power. He concentrated on the exploitation of the common person by doctors, religious frauds, and the pedants in society and presented his criticisms in his comedy.

Les Precieuses Ridicules, 1659

By contrast, Jean Racine was considered to be the quintessential neoclassical tragic writer, and his play *Phèdre* was considered to be the quintessential neoclassical play. Neoclassicism refers to a very distinct movement in the visual, decorative, written, and performed arts that received its influence from the artists of the ancient Greek and Roman periods and particularly the writings by Aristotle (*Poetics*) and Horace (*The Art of Poetry*). The neoclassical period was in vogue from the middle of the seventeenth century until well into the eighteenth century and, for the purposes of theatre, consisted of very strict rules and practices.

In brief, plays had to be written within a five-act play structure. They had to follow the unities of time, place and action, that is, assuming a twenty-four hour day, all action and movement within the play could only include what could reasonably be expected during a twenty-four hour period. There was no violence on stage, plays had to have "purity of form" or decorum—only royal or upper class characters could appear in tragedy, while lower class characters appeared in comedies—and the forms were distinct unto themselves; there were no tragicomedies. There was a need for verisimilitude or an appearance of truth. This meant that there were not any more soliloquies—if a character was going to perform a long speech, s/he had to have another character onstage as a confidant.

Inaugural of the Salle du Palais-Cardinal, W.D. Howarth, 1641

The neoclassical movement was present across Europe in varying degrees throughout the seventeenth and eighteenth centuries; as noted, it was "perfected" in France; on the other hand, it was not considered of great importance in Britain. It was a style that emphasized form over content, and many playwrights and theatre practitioners found it too limiting.

By the time the period known officially as the Restoration was over, at the beginning of the eighteenth century, there was a change of mood and ethos occurring in England that found its way into the writing of the new century.

There were two distinct classes of this era—the aristocrats and the *nouveau riche*. London itself was seen to be a center for the aristocracy, at this time a small, tightly knit community. London was a place that exhibited leading examples of fashion and taste; this was believed to be the reason that a majority of the leisured class was attracted to it. Once in London, a large percentage of the aristocracy would meet in places such as private drawing rooms, public promenades or chocolate houses. Outwardly, these would appear to be harmless social gatherings, where people would discuss political, philosophical or moral issues, but enjoyed conversing on the trivialities of life and anecdotes about character. Two characteristic examples of contemporary discussion, cited in T. H. White's essay, *Royal Gossip*, are the nature of the "bootikins" worn by Horace Walpole for his gout or what Dr. Johnson used to do with his dried orange peel. The interest in a person's character, however, often took them down the rocky path toward gossip and scandal. The contemporary newspaper, *The Gazette* (1774), likened the virulence of scandal and gossip during this age to a "horrid monster," and essayist Thomas Carlyle often referred to this period as "the age of prose, lying, of sham, the fraudulent bankrupt century, the reign of Beelzebub, the peculiar era of cant."

Ada Rehan as Lady Teazle in *The School for Scandal*, Ian van Beers, 1893

LAURIE J. WOLF

Although he was referring to the salacious hunger for scandal evident in this age, this is not to assume that scandal is indigenous only to the eighteenth century. Playwrights have always seen scandal as an interesting issue. This is evident in the work of William Congreve. In his play *The Way of the World*, the character of Fainall describes to Mirabell the "cabal nights" that are organized by Lady Wishfort. These "cabal nights" mirror the scandalous gatherings of influential people from both the Restoration and the eighteenth century.

A parallel situation happens in a play called *The School for Scandal* (1777) by Richard Brinsley Sheridan (1751-1816). The character of Snake within Sheridan's play is almost the prototype of our modern "gossip" columnist and the coven of scandal mongers at the beginning of the play are the equivalents of the tabloids and media of today where, as Sir Peter says in *The School for Scandal*, "a character [is] dead at every word."

Both the aristocrats who frequented the "cabal nights" and the newspapers of today thrive on ruined reputations and the ensuing hypocrisy, resulting from the disparity between public reputations and private realities. Sheridan and the other playwrights whose works marked the Restoration and eighteenth century were eminently aware of the differences between public virtue and private realities. They were aware that a person would often want to be seen in a way that was not true to their actual behavior, and it was those differences that characterized the late Restoration and eighteenth century. Once exposed, those inconsistencies were used by scandalmongers and gossips to ruin many people. The political contradictions that were manifested at the beginning of the seventeenth century following the accession of James I to the English throne, began to permeate all levels of society, and, as always, the stage was an accurate barometer of social ills and trends.

Play for Study: Aphra Behn's The Rover

Aphra Behn's *The Rover* is a model play of the Restoration period. It contains all the devices that were common to the majority of Restoration playwrights, such as the use of sexual situations, banished cavaliers, disguise and mistaken identity and the use of the Spanish influence. One of the best ways to guarantee a Restoration audience's attention was with the use of sex; in *The Rover*, Mrs. Behn makes frequent use of this belief. Every scene with Willmore, the Rover, is filled with sexual innuendo. There are a number of scenes with Ned Blunt, beginning with his infatuation with

Lucetta, the prostitute, who seduces and then robs him, and continuing to the end, where he fantasizes about overpowering and raping Florinda. Interspersed with these scenes are a myriad of others that deal with the men procuring prostitutes, and the women trying to find lovers for themselves.

Aphra Behn, George Scharf, 19th Century

The theme of the banished cavaliers was very topical at the time. These men, defined as "adherents of Charles I," shared the displaced king's wandering on the continent. The fact that *The Rover*, subtitled *The Banished Cavaliers*, and that Thomas Killigrew's *Thomaso or The Wanderer* was the source for Mrs. Behn's play, demonstrates the influence that these wanderers had on the popular playwrights.

The device of disguise and mistaken identity are used to their fullest extent in *The Rover*. The play takes place in "Naples, at Carnival Time." Setting the play during a time in which disguise was the order of the day not only conformed to Restoration convention, but also allowed the plot of *The Rover* to develop to its greatest potential. The crux of the plotting by Hellena, Florinda, and Valeria would be unable to proceed without this masking device.

The Spanish influence was extremely vital in the development of this play. Not only did it lend credibility to the scenes of the Carnival, a traditional festival in Spain, but also it gave a sense of displacement to the cavaliers. In the whole range of English history, there is no other period when dramatists turned more frequently to Spain for sources and formal models.

Another reason for placing *The Rover* in the world of a Spanish colony is for the purpose of distancing the action from Aphra Behn's England. She places the women's departure from the standards of accepted behavior in a locale that is both foreign and familiar to British audiences, allowing her thesis to be presented under the guise of a foreign problem. This was not a device that was unique to Restoration writers; playwrights had, for many years, set their works in lands foreign to their own, which allowed a greater scope of criticism toward their own societies.

We see a similar sense of distancing in the use of masks. Mrs. Behn has her characters conduct the majority of their business from behind masks, leading to an overwhelming incidence of pretext and mistaken identity. The dominant ideology of her world was one of repression and subordination of its women. Despite the revolutionary actions of the women in the play, Mrs. Behn is still not offering any real solutions to the problem; it remains, causing an ongoing tension throughout the action. The use of masks exacerbates this tension by never allowing the characters to achieve the sense of freedom that is gained when an identity is known and can be taken for granted and, therefore, exploited.

For Further Reading:

G Blakemore Evans. *Elizabethan Jacobean Drama: The Theatre in Its Time.* New York: New Amsterdam Books, 1998.

Janet Clare. *Art Made Tongue-Tied by Authority: Elizabethan and Jacobean Dramatic Censorship.* Manchester: Manchester University Press, 1999.

Melveena McKendrick. *Theatre in Spain, 1490-1700.* Cambridge: Cambridge University Press, 1989.

Robert D Hume. *The London Theatre World, 1660-1800.* Carbondale: Southern Illinois University Press, 1980.

CHAPTER 9

GERMAN AND ENGLISH ROMANTICISM AND ENGLISH MELODRAMA

AS WE DISCUSSED in chapter 8, the movement of art known as Neoclassicism lasted from the middle of the seventeenth century until the end of the eighteenth century. Neoclassicism took its influence from Aristotle's *Poetics* and Horace's *Art of Poetry*; there were a number of interpretations and variations about what the classical poets meant, but the major characteristics that were followed in the late seventeen and early eighteenth centuries by primarily the Italians and especially the French were these:

- Verisimilitude—an appearance of truth
- Five-act structure
- Three unities—time, space, action
- Use of confidant—instead of soliloquy and chorus
- No violence on stage
- Decorum—appropriateness, no individualized character types, codification of humanity according to class, age, gender, profession, and rank
- Purity of form

  - Comedy—middle or lower class, domestic/private affairs, happy endings, everyday speech
  - Tragedy—ruling class, based on history or mythology, unhappy endings, lofty or poetic style

These constrictions became an individual's reality, e.g., form as an outward manifestation of an inner idea. Neoclassicism was based in large part on the premise that one could discover, through rational analysis, adequate criteria for everything in life or literature.

Morning in the Tropics, Fredrick Edwin Church, circa 1858

For all of its intentions, Neoclassicism began to lose its following as the eighteenth century wore on. Between the American and the French Revolutions, in addition to the Germanic states fighting amongst themselves, Neoclassicism was seen as another form of repressive practice. Artists began turning more and more toward the natural world for inspiration and that proved to be the beginning of Romanticism.

There were a number of forces that led the way to the Romantic Movement. There was a growing distrust of reason as the principle tool for achieving a human being's highest goals. In the mid to latter part of the eighteenth century, that view was gradually replaced by trust in natural instinct as a guide to correct feelings and actions.

The general doubt about the suitability of the existing social and political order increased as the rise of the middle class prompted a reconsideration of the distinctions that made the majority subservient to an aristocratic minority. The equality of all people and freedom of action were the major themes of the new movement; it is easy to see the correlation between this manner of thinking and the nationalistic fervor behind both the American and French Revolutions.

The Neoclassical idea that truth is to be defined within rules was replaced by the conviction that truth could only be discovered in the infinite variety of creation. In other words, according to the Romantics, God created the universe out of himself. Therefore, everything in existence is part of everything else. To know ultimate truth, one must know as much of creation as possible.

The Romantics believed that since all creation has a common origin, a thorough and careful study of any part might lead to a glimpse of the whole. For example, when examining aspects of nature—trees, grass or mountains reflect something about human beings and in return, human beings reflect something about them. The more unspoiled something is and the less it deviates from its natural state, the more suitable it is in the search for truth.

Romantic writers showed a marked preference for poetry about natural objects and landscapes as well as for drama about unspoiled men living in primitive times or those in rebellion against restraints imposed by society. They believed that since the ultimate source of creation was God, the truth was infinite and beyond total comprehension or adequate expression. Therefore, it is impossible to ever grasp all of reality, although one should continually try to do so.

Illuminatenhöhle, Eugen Lennhoff, 1931

LAURIE J. WOLF

In the Romantic view, the person most capable of grasping and expressing truth is the genius. This was directly opposed to Neoclassicism, where the belief was, if a writer followed the rules, then good drama would be produced. At the end of the eighteenth century, there was the need for some special, indefinable quality—the quality of genius. The Romantics believed that genius was thought to include an intuitive ability to grasp the greatness of the universe; this capacity removed the individual able to perceive this from ordinary people, who were supposedly caught up in the everyday, material world and seemingly blind to their true natures. A genius was therefore seen as different and, at times, in conflict with the rest of the world.

The artist was expected to search for forms, which were adequate to the expression of great truths. New forms needed to allow maximum freedom in trying to explore the infinity of Creation. Shakespeare's plays came to represent the ideal form in the Romantic period, just as Greek and Roman drama had served as models for writers of the neoclassical era.

As a deliberate movement, Romanticism began in Germany, although many of its concepts had been developing there and elsewhere for some time. The German romantic writers were not as much in revolt as later French writers were to be; they saw themselves as clarifying and developing concepts derived from the *Sturm und Drang* (Storm and Stress) school of thought.

Sturm und Drang was the experimental movement of young writers in revolt against eighteenth century rationalism, which lasted over a twenty-year period from 1767 until 1787, described as completely formless rebellions against neoclassicism (particularly because of Goethe's *Götz Von Berlichingen* with fifty-four scenes). Most of the plays were written with five acts and as many observe the unities of time and place as those that violate them. Since they never agreed upon an alternative philosophy, the plays showed wide variations both in thought and expression; much of the subject matter was considered shocking. To give two examples:

- Jacob Lenz's *The Soldiers* proposed a state-sponsored system of prostitution so as to protect respectable young women from seduction by soldiers; and
- Heinrich Wagner's *The Child Murderess*—a rape occurs just off stage and a baby is killed on stage by a hatpin through its brain.

Two of the most important dramatists of the period were Johann Wolfgang von Goethe (1749-1832) and Johann Christoph Friedrich von

Schiller (1759-1805), both of whom denied being Romanticists; however, both wrote plays which helped to establish the new drama, and those playwrights who did consider themselves part of the Romantic movement acknowledged their debt to the work of Goethe and Schiller. Both writers argued that drama should transform ordinary experience rather than create an illusion of real life. They adopted verse, conventionalized structural patterns, simple but harmonious settings and costumes, and precise rhythmic speech. With these techniques, they attempted to lead spectators beyond their normal perceptions into the realm of ideal truth.

During this time, the last vestiges of Neoclassicism almost wholly disappeared under the onslaught of Romanticism. In some countries, the romantic ideal was self-consciously followed, and in others it was hardly known; but almost everywhere, the melodramatic and pseudo-Shakespearean mode in playwriting, historical accuracy in settings and costumes, and emotional and psychological realism in acting had made themselves felt and had combined to create a theatre by 1850 that was unlike anything in the previous century.

The most striking changes in the eighteenth century theatre occurred in the Germanic territories. In 1700, Germany was composed of many small states divided by religious and political differences. The Thirty Years' War (1618-1648) had depleted both its population and its resources, leaving few large cities and little wealth. Theatre was divided between private court productions and public travelling companies, with little connection between the two. Court theatres developed under the influence of Italian opera, and after 1652, the court at Vienna became one of the major theatrical centers of Europe; its example was imitated throughout Germany.

The real founders of the professional German stage were the touring companies. The first travelling players came from England around 1590, but gradually, Germans replaced the English actors. None of the troupes had a permanent base since no town could afford to support a professional company, and because of this, touring was necessary—but it was very costly and time consuming.

The low state of the theatre was reflected in the plays, which featured violent action, exaggerated characters and bombastic dialogue. There was a clownish stock character, Hanswurst, who was a character based on Arlecchino of the Commedia dell'Arte. This character played a major role in all plays, even the serious works.

All of these factors worked toward keeping the German theatre in low repute until after 1725 when Johann Gottsched (1700-1766) and

Carolina Neuber (1699-1760) made the first serious effort to reform the German stage. Gottsched, who was interested in improving the level of German literature and in elevating taste and morals, formed a liaison with Neuber's acting troupe. His standards were derived almost entirely from French neoclassical drama, which was completely unknown to audiences of popular German theatre.

Hanswurst-Koeln, F.X. Schlösser, 1831

Neuber wanted to raise the level of acting and the reputation of the theatrical profession by insisting on careful rehearsals and a high level of personal morality. One of her first acts was to get rid of the character of Hanswurst, and she revised her repertory to bring it closer to Gottsched's aims. She was not entirely successful, however, her work, along with that of Gottsched, marked the turning point in the German theatre.

Germany's first important dramatist was Gotthold Lessing (1729-1781). He turned attention away from French neoclassicism to English drama as being more compatible with German tastes. His play, *Miss Sara Sampson* (1755), set in England, established the vogue for domestic tragedy in Germany. Lessing's critical writings, especially the Hamburg Dramaturgy (1767-1768) (the first writing on the work of a dramaturge in performance) also helped to turn attention away from French drama and to establish more defensible standards appropriate to the German theatre.

The first of the German National Theatres was established at Gotha in 1775. Other theatres at Vienna, Mannheim, Cologne, Weimar and Berlin followed this. By 1800, almost every German capital had a state theatre organized along the lines of the Comedie Francaise. The German theatre had undergone an extreme revolution. Permanent theatres had their own resident companies. Thanks to the work of Carolina Neuber and Johann Gottsched, the acting profession was respected, and German drama was beginning to assume international importance. In addition, Germany was in the process of developing a romantic drama that would overthrow those neoclassical ideals that dominated the stages of Europe for more than a century and a half.

Melodrama

Melodrama, Honorè Daumier, circa 1858

Melodrama was considered to be one of the most popular forms of entertainment during the nineteenth century. The name was originally derived from the Greek (melody and drama) and means "music drama." It developed from the French form of *mélodrame*, the exceptional success of which was due to the writings of Rene Charles Guilbert de Pixérécourt (1773-1844), a prolific playwright and director who was said to write almost exclusively for the illiterate and lower classes.

There were many different forms of melodrama, but most of them had elements in common. They tended to feature sensational plots, with a small number of stock characters: the villain, the heroine, the hero, an aging parent, and a comic character, all involved in scenarios based around the themes of love and murder. Very often, the not very bright hero finds himself duped by the scheming villain who wants the heroine for himself. Fate will usually intervene at the last moment, the villain will be thwarted, and the hero and heroine will live happily ever after, proving that good does triumph over evil.

There were also some very specific genres of melodrama. Gothic melodrama, which became popular in the latter part of the eighteenth century and early nineteenth century, contained the basic melodramatic components, although the desire for spectacle spiked sharply upward with this particular style. One of the main aspects of Gothic melodrama was to arouse horror and fear, and the storylines, settings and the "natural" elements were directed toward that goal. Graveyards, ruined abbeys, moors, dungeons and forests were all popular scenic settings for various plot devices.

There were many supernatural elements, especially in plays that featured monsters (think of Mary Shelley's *Frankenstein* (1818) or some other nonhuman fiend with terrifying powers who was determined to make the lives of the hero and heroine more trying than usual; vampires were very popular. Ghosts would turn up quite frequently in Gothic melodrama (with appropriate special effects), usually at the worst possible moment for the villain (ghosts were almost always on the side of goodness). This genre was the forerunner to our modern horror film in many ways—both visually and in the narrative.

Character stereotypes were very much the same as in other melodramas, but the villain, who was always a threatening and powerful figure, was especially so in Gothic melodrama. The terror and movement of the play was always centered with the villain, and he was so all-powerful, that it was always a mystery as to how and why he was defeated.

Nautical and military melodrama was primarily an English phenomenon. Because Britain was and is an island nation and during the nineteenth century the phrase, "the sun never sets on the British Empire" was still true, dramatists had a never-ending supply of possible scenarios from which to draw inspiration. There were always many celebrations of patriotism occurring, and men were constantly leaving and returning home to waiting wives and families. Additionally, the hatred and contempt for the enemy and glorification of the British military easily made the transition to the hero and villain characters. Writers were onto a good thing; as long as Britain was involved in fighting somewhere, there was always a potential story for a play. And even if there were not any conflicts currently being resolved, historical battles could be fought all over again. It was the biggest and most obvious display of dramatic jingoism until the studios began making films about the Second World War, cashing in on the overwhelming wave of nationalism.

The label, Domestic Melodrama, is a bit of a misnomer because it covered such a broad area of topics. It may have encompassed situations of village or farm life, which focused on the foibles of a farmer, an evil landlord or squire, a wayward daughter, an honest workman or peasant. On the other hand, it also included situations of city life, which showed the hardship of life in the city, e.g., working in a factory, crime, gambling, or drinking and its consequences.

Audiences were shown familiar situations that they encountered on a daily basis, but the staged event was heightened for dramatic purposes. For example:

- Sinister temptations put in the way of the hero, with extra dangers for the heroine.
- Many heroines abducted or lured to London under false pretenses.
- Feminine distress—The heroine is reduced to begging and starving in the street, usually in a snowstorm and often with cold, hungry, and sick children.
- The hero suffered from the vice of gambling. The plays would dwell on the distress and poverty caused to loved ones, especially if they were wives and children. These plays usually included a realistic gambling scene.

Temperance melodramas were among the most popular forms of domestic melodrama. Temperance workers believed that a worse temptation than gambling was drinking.

Sometimes drinking would triumph, and the family would be destroyed in some terrible tragedy. An example of this can be seen in Tom Taylor's *The Bottle*: A factory worker loses his job, gambles away all his money, his furniture is repossessed, he is kicked out of his house and is reduced to begging on the street, his youngest child dies of starvation, his oldest son apprenticed to criminals, he kills his wife in a drunken rage, and he ends up in chains in a madhouse.

This situation seems over the top now, but in the nineteenth century, the playwright, actors, and audience took this very seriously. Alcoholism was a severe problem, both in Britain and in the United States. Starting from around 1830, temperance organizations were working full-time to try to stop people from drinking. Melodrama as a form was ideally suited to moral admonition; the moral imperative within the play was usually delivered in the form of a lecture by actual temperance spokespeople to both the character and the theatre audience—another indicator that melodrama was a fairly accurate social reflector of its times.

Henry Irving-*Vanity Fair,* Carlo Pellegrini, 1874

Although melodrama continued throughout the nineteenth century as popular entertainment, beginning in the 1850s and 1860s, there was a gradual return of a bourgeois audience, leading to the further development of "society melodrama," melodramatic plays that dealt with characters from a higher echelon of society. The sources of the plays changed as well. After hundreds of plays that dealt with the working class, novels began to take on an improved status in society and became sources for their own types of plays. Action returned to the drawing room, and the return of the middle and upper classes was encouraged—both on the stage and in the audience.

Many of the melodramatic styles that were most popular in the nineteenth century have been adapted for our popular culture. The vampires of Gothic melodrama have found a new life in the *Twilight* series and other books and movies of that genre. Romantic love stories we see in the movies and on television are as melodramatic as they come. And docudramas like *Band of Brothers* and *Pacific* featuring soldiers and events from the Second World War are very close, both stylistically and in intent to nautical melodrama.

For Further Reading:

David Grimstead. *Melodrama Unveiled.* Chicago: University of Chicago press, 1968.

George Rowell. *The Victorian Theatre.* Cambridge: Cambridge University Press, 1978.

Michael R Booth. *English Plays of the Nineteenth Century: Pantomimes, Extravaganzas and Burlesques.* Oxford: Oxford University Press, 1976.

Oscar Brockett and Robert Findlay. *Century of Innovation.* Boston: Allyn and Bacon, 1991.

CHAPTER 10

THE MODERN PERIOD: REALISMS AND ANTIREALISMS

M OST CONTEMPORARY THEATRE practitioners would agree that the term "modern" applies to the perceptions, movements and techniques in drama and theatre that emerged during the nineteenth century and developed during the twentieth century, i.e., Naturalism, Realism, Symbolism, Dadaism, Surrealism, Expressionism, and Absurdism. There were numerous developments and inventions occurring during this time frame that led to the evolution of modern thought.

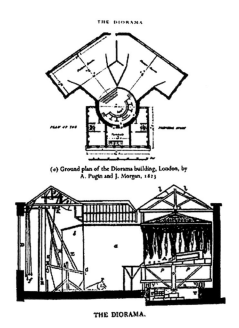

Diorama diagram, 1823

The Industrial Revolution was the period of time, beginning in the eighteenth century during when vast changes were made in production and manufacturing. The movement started in Great Britain and eventually spread to the rest of Europe and North America. It led to tremendous modifications in mining, agriculture and transport and had a profound effect on the way ordinary people led their lives.

A major change came with the establishment of factories. This meant a large-scale displacement of great numbers of people to be nearer the workplace, leading to urbanization. With urbanization came other problems, mostly seen in overcrowding in town centers, leading to slum conditions, crime and corruption.

This was all happening at a time when governments were least equipped to deal with this new set of problems. Memories of the French and American Revolutions haunted Europe throughout much of the first half of the nineteenth century; governments were trying to ensure that events like these wouldn't recur and to this end, they failed to distinguish between legitimate demands for social reforms and revolutionary politics. By 1850, it had become evident that more democratic political systems were needed. This recognition led to a trend for playwrights to deal with lower classes as dramatic subjects in serious plays for really the first time

There was a lot of questioning of past practices in all areas of society. The population of the nineteenth century was known for its fascination with anything perceived to be, however remotely, scientific. This provided a sympathetic audience for new ideas, no matter in what form they were presented.

There were several theorists and practitioners whose work contributed to this new mind-set:

- Auguste Comte (1798-1857)—considered the father of Sociology; he believed that by applying scientific method (observation, hypothesis, and analysis) to social problems, the causes could be determined and effects controlled.
- Charles Darwin (1809-1882)—*The Origin of the Species* (1859); role of God/Divine Providence reduced; the place of human beings in the universe was seriously altered, e.g., the human race was changeable.
- Karl Marx (1818-1883)—*The Communist Manifesto*; outlined shift of power from aristocrats to working class; the worker provided the basis for Realism; Brecht's *The Mother*, Hauptmann's *The Weavers*.
- Louis Daguerre (1787-1851)—Known for the invention of the daguerreotype process of photography; visual realism.
- Sigmund Freud (1856-1939)—Psychoanalysis; led the way to a closer examination of characters as individuals, rather than stereotypes.

At the same time, there were some very significant changes in theatrical practices. There was the gradual abandonment of the repertory system. Since the audience sizes had increased, the theatre owners opted for longer runs of plays, leading to a reduction in the number of plays required. Following in the footsteps of Georg II, Duke of Saxe-Meinengen, there was the emergence of the director as the dominant artistic force in the theatre, thereby nearly destroying the actor-manager system. Theatres started to add electric lighting as it became available and to increase their technical capabilities.

One of the most prolific playwrights during the first half of the century had been Eugene Scribe (1761-1891). Between 1811 and 1861, he wrote over three hundred pieces for the Parisian theatre. He is best remembered for the "well-made play" formula, which, unfortunately, nowadays is often used as a term of derision. However, the well-made play was a combination of dramatic devices:

- Careful exposition and preparation
- Cause to effect arrangement of incidents
- Building scenes to a climax
- Use of withheld information, startling reversals, and suspense

Publicitè pour Thérèsè Raquin, circa 1877

The plays now appear shallow by modern standards because characterization and thought were sacrificed to devices and intrigue, but they were incredibly popular with audiences in their own time.

In contrast, there was a developing body of thought in opposition to this unreal and fairly comfortable form of writing, a form of drama known as Naturalism. A French writer by the name of Emile Zola was the primary force of Naturalism. His main interest was in the novel, but he also wanted to reform theatre, which he considered to be fifty years behind the novel. Naturalism, as envisioned by Zola, was a drama of observation and scientific fact. He believed that, in order to write a play, a dramatist only had to reproduce a "slice of life," the truthful reproduction of life on stage. This was not a long-lasting form of drama; for one thing, it had the tendency to be terribly boring. Imagine that you are sitting in your classroom, listening to your professor droning on, and someone comes along and removes a wall and places an audience where the wall once was. Nothing else changes. That is the "slice of life" that Zola was talking about. Another problem with the plays of Naturalism was that they were unremittingly grim. These works showed the sordidness of life in all of its manifestations. A good example of a Naturalistic work is Maxim Gorki's *The Lower Depths* (1901):

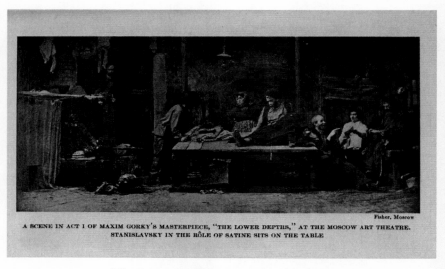

A SCENE IN ACT 1 OF MAXIM GORKY'S MASTERPIECE, "THE LOWER DEPTHS," AT THE MOSCOW ART THEATRE. STANISLAVSKY IN THE RÔLE OF SATINE SITS ON THE TABLE

The Lower Depths, Maxim Gorky, 1922

Maxim Gorki's *The Lower Depths*

The play is set in a flophouse in Moscow at the turn of the nineteenth century. It is a place of extremes. On the one hand, it is a refuge for the destitute, suffering and dying; on the other, a place for survivors, the perverse and self-preservers. Included in this group are a thief, a gambler, an ex-artist, an ex-aristocrat and a prostitute. All of them had at one time an ambition, a goal, but because of their lack of will and the injustice and cruelty of the world, they were forced into the depths and cast back whenever they attempted to rise. They are the superfluous ones, dehumanized and brutalized. Into this pit of humanity comes Luka, a traveler, probably on the run (he has no papers). He is wily and shrewd, he lives on his wits and is a survivor, but he is also kind. Unable to pass suffering by, he offers his "consoling lies"—he comforts Anna, dying of tuberculosis, with promise of heaven and tantalizes an alcoholic, out-of-work actor, Satine, with talk of a cure in some remote clinic. His words bring instant calm and hope. Other characters, trapped in a life of poverty, dislike his temporary comforting, calling him a liar. They prefer to justify their aimless existences by the hopelessness, both theological and social, of their situation.

Following the deaths of several of the residents of the house, the play ends, but the indictment of society is clear. The so-called depravity and crimes of the derelicts are fundamentally the depravity and criminal antisocial attitude of society itself that first creates the underworld and having created it, wastes much energy and effort in suppressing and destroying the menacing phantom of its own making; blind to the value of the individual and ignorant of the beautiful possibilities inherent in even the most despised children of the depths.

Following on from Naturalism was the style known as Realism. Henrik Ibsen (1828-1906), a Norwegian playwright who was writing at roughly the same time as Zola, has been called the "Father of Modern Realism," although not all of Ibsen's plays can be considered realistic. His main plays, *A Doll's House, Ghosts, Hedda Gabler*, and *An Enemy of the People* fall into this genre, however, many others have a heightened poetic to them.

The situation is similar with August Strindberg (1849-1912). Writing in Sweden from about 1870, he was a die-hard fan of Zola. He wrote a preface to his one-act play, *Miss Julie*, discussing how naturalistic it was, but even with *Miss Julie* and certainly his later plays, such as *The Ghost Sonata*, he moved well out of the realm of realism and into symbolism and surrealism.

Anton Chekhov (1860-1904), writing in Russia, and George Bernard Shaw (1854-1950), writing in England, are two other "Classical Realists" whose names you may have heard.

One of the main differences between Naturalism and Realism was that the first presented the problem (almost always a social issue) as it was. It did not offer any sort of solution because the writer did not believe that there was one. What was important was to make the problem known, as clearly and dispassionately as possible.

Realism, by contrast, presented many of the same concerns. However, the topics were mediated by a dramatic storyline with characters to which one could empathize. Very often, the results were the same as with Naturalism, however, options had been presented to the characters and they made informed choices as to whether or not they followed a new path or stayed with the old.

Naturalism and Realism also had detractors; there were many dramatists who believed that a naturalistic or realistic approach was capable of revealing only one part of the truth, that which can be perceived by the five senses. These antirealistic dramatists believed that the more significant aspects of truth could be found in mystery and myth and in dreams rather than in the material world. These practitioners advocated a drama composed of images and symbols and a theatre in which line, color and mood would replace illusionistic recreations of real places. A short description of the major movement follows.

Symbolism

The symbolists believed that poetic language and imagery took precedence over all else. Symbolism, as a movement was launched in 1885 with a manifesto written by Jean Moréas. Stéphane Mallarmé became the recognized leader, although opinions were often widely divergent. Mallarmé believed that only the poet could reveal the mystery of the universe through his perception of analogies and correspondence between the visible and invisible realms of being.

He considered drama an essentially sacred and mysterious rite, which, through dream, reverie, allusion and musicality, one could evoke the hidden spiritual meanings of existence. The salient characteristics of Mallarmé's aesthetic include:

- Drama is the expression of inner life.
- Drama is the expression of mystery: the revelation of the hidden wonder of the universe.

- The language of drama is poetry rather than prose, evocative rather than descriptive and relies upon suggestion as opposed to statement.
- The stage is detheatricalized, reduced to the barest and simplest elements of histrionic performance.
- The theatre brings into play all of the arts, interrelated within a poetic structure.

Not all symbolists agreed with Mallarmé's ideas, but they affected nearly all.

Dadaism

The Dadaists believed that art should mirror the madness of the world. The movement was started in Zurich by Tristan Tzara, among other significant artists, during the last years of World War I. The movement was named "Dada," a nonsense or baby-talk term, thereby indicating the certainty that European culture had lost any real meaning. The artists, refugees from the war, set out in their bitterness to mock all the values of shat they believed to be a culture gone mad. Since the artists' intentions were fundamentally nihilistic, Dada works are difficult to interpret and are best approached with their creators' avowed spirit of nonart or even antiart in mind, "Dada is against everything, even Dada."

Première *Ubu Roi,* Alfred Jarry, 1922

The playwright that the Dadaists adopted was Alfred Jarry, whose play *Ubu Roi* was anarchic in the extreme and convinced many critics that Jarry was the father of the Absurdist movement. *Ubu Roi* (translated as *King Ubu* and *King Turd*) is Jarry's most famous work. *Ubu Roi* eliminates most of the dramatic action from its text and uses scatological humor and farce to present Jarry's views on art, literature, politics, the ruling classes, and current events, vividly illustrated by the play's first word, "*Merdre!*"

Surrealism

The surrealists believed that the subconscious mind was the source of the artist's most significant perceptions. They thought that the truth was most apt to surface when the superego's censorship and the ego's logic had been neutralized. Surrealist artists and writers gained their effects most often by mingling the familiar and the strange, as in Salvador Dali's melting clocks. The surrealist manifesto, in which he defined surrealism as "pure psychic automatism," was written by André Breton (1896-1966) in 1924. He believed in the primacy of the subconscious and stated that in moments of truth, life's contradictions are transcended.

Notrica Thirty Second Street Market, Paul Torres, 2009

Expressionism

Expressionism was one of the primary movements after the First World War. It was initially given significance as an artistic label in France around

1901, in order to distinguish the kind of painting that was being produced by Van Gogh, Gauguin, and others from the works of the impressionist painters. The Impressionists sought to capture the appearance of objects as seen under a certain light at a particular moment, while the Expressionists emphasized strong inner feelings about objects and portrayed life as modified and distorted by the painter's own vision of reality.

Around 1910-1911, the term was introduced into Germany where it was picked up by critics and was popularized as a label for modes of production already in existence in literature and visual arts. Although it was bound to be a catchall term that applied to many different examples, there were several points that most expressionists agreed upon:

> Most were opposed to realism/naturalism because those movements glorified science, which the expressionists associated with technology and industrialization.

They disliked naturalism's emphasis on external appearance, which they considered an insignificant aspect of reality.

They were contemptuous of new romanticism. They believed that it avoided contemporary social problems.

There were some very specific goals of Expressionism:

- Dramas were primarily message-centered; organized through idea, theme or motif, rather than cause and effect.
- Characters were mostly impersonal figures.
- The central character was usually sacrificed to the materialism, hypocrisy or callousness of other characters, which epitomize various social attitudes and human types.

Each element was reduced to its essentials:

- Plot—might be a mere demonstration of a thesis or argument
- Characters—generic
- Dialogue—drastically reduced; sometimes only one—to two-word sentences, telegraph style
- Use of aural/visual distortion
- Use of light

Walls might lean inward to suggest oppression; trees become skeletons as precursors of death

Bizarre events would occur—corpses would rise from graves, groups of identical characters would appear in various places

There would be sharp contrasts in form—dialogue might alternate between prose/poetry; idyllic passages/obscenities; telegraphic speech/lengthy monologues

The works were permeated with a sense of dreamlike fantasy and magic

The overall impression was of an allegory clothed in nightmare or vision

Theatre of the Absurd

The term, Absurdism, was coined by the critic, Martin Esslin (1918-2002), around 1960 to describe the work of several dramatists who had come to prominence during the preceding decade. Those writers that Esslin was referring to were united by a shared view—that ideas about man's significance and behavior are equally illogical. To the Absurdists, ultimate truth is the chaos, contradictions and inanities that make up daily existence; it encompasses the lack of logic, order and certainty.

Waiting for Godot in Doon School, Merlay Samuel, 2011

Existentialism was one of the most significant forerunners of Absurdism. As a movement, it attracted international attention after the Second World War.

The two central problems in existential philosophy are:

What does "to exist" mean?
What does this imply about action?

The most well known existentialist dramatists were Jean-Paul Sartre (1905-1980) and Albert Camus (1913-1960). Sartre said that in all his work, he attempted to draw logical conclusions from a consistent atheism. He believed that there were no absolute moral values and that man was adrift in a world devoid of purpose; therefore, each person is free (since they are not bound to a god or a set of verifiable standards) and is responsible only to himself. Camus's theory was that absurdity arises from the gulf between man's aspirations and the meaningless universe into which he has been thrust.

The Absurdists differed from Sartre and Camus in two major respects: the Absurdists emphasized the absurdity of existence rather than the necessity of bringing order to absurdity; and they embodied their chaotic subjects in a form which abandoned the logical cause to effect arrangement for one based on themes and associations. These ideas may be clarified by the listing of the characteristics of Absurdism below:

Definition of Absurd

"Out of harmony with reason or propriety; incongruous, unreasonable, illogical."

In terms of theatre, "Absurd is that which is devoid of purpose . . . cut off from his religious, metaphysical, and transcendental roots, man is lost; all his actions become senseless, absurd, useless." (Eugene Ionesco, 1909-1994)

Characteristics of Absurdism

A. Traditional pattern of cause and effect abandoned.
B. Characters tend toward typical or archetypal, instead of specific and individual; will occasionally exchange roles or metamorphose into another character.
C. Time and place are generalized; play often occurs in a symbolic location or in a void or in limbo.
D. Language is, for the most part, downgraded; they talk just as much, but recognize it as if in a game—audience perceives the silliness of it.

E. Spectacle is usually used symbolically or metaphorically to compensate in part for demotion of language.

F. Traditional distinction among dramatic forms disappears; serious becomes grotesque and comic takes on tragic overtones.

World War II created a crisis of conscience among intellectuals, but because traditional values seemed incapable of coping with such dilemmas, writers looked for alternative methods, such as Theatre of the Absurd.

As a final thought on the overall modern period, here is a word on postmodernism. The different aspects of modernism that you have just read about deal with the quest for truth, in all its various forms, but for the most part, the forms have been mainly organic.

The postmodernists have elected to transcend or dismiss the individual quest for truth. Modernism's organic theories are considered to be too limiting and fixed, offering little assistance to a postmodern artist whose vision thrives on dissociation, fragmentation, and a meaningless universe.

Postmodernists like Robert Wilson, Anne Bogart, Peter Sellars, and Robert LePage challenge the artist's interpretive ability to recreate a truthful representation of a historical period or style. Instead, they have turned to their interpretation of an imagistic/metaphorical theatre to explore new ways to perceive the play's dramatic world. As an example, a postmodern artist will sometimes deconstruct a play text to extract what they perceive to be the play's true meaning.

A case in point would be the Wooster Group, who is known for their deconstructions and adaptations of existing work. They took the text of Arthur Miller's *The Crucible*, which is a play that historicizes the seventeenth century Salem witch trials by commenting overtly on the political climate in America during the 1950s, in particular, Senator Joseph McCarthy's attack on would-be Communists.

The Wooster Group's adaptation is called *LSD (Just the High Points)* and in this play they historicize Miller's play by subjecting it to a postmodern political critique that evokes Timothy Leary, Alan Ginsburg, G. Gordon Liddy and other writers and politicians of the 1950s and 1960s.

Each text in some way undermines the others, with the result that no one method of verifying history, of re-presenting it, is privileged. The performance itself is interrogated and revealed as a distortion or a hallucination. Postmodern work is a very self-reflexive method; think of the difference between modernisms and postmodernisms. Modernism is predicated on scientific observation and replication, while Postmodernism examines and deconstructs that methodology, in order to expose the processes that suppress difference, manipulates presence and its authority and restrains any kind of marginal or subversive activity.

Play for Study: Henrik Ibsen's A Doll's House

One of the unique aspects of *A Doll's House* is that the play is deceptively simple, but the dramatic structure is more complex.

Nazimova, in *A Dolls House,* 1922

The plot is based on a secret known to the audience but withheld from certain characters. In this case, Nora's fraudulent loan is the secret that is kept from all the characters except Krogstad and Mrs. Linde.

The intensity of the action and suspense steadily builds as characters introduce exposition and utilize devices such as entrances and exits, letters, etc. In this play, the appearance of Krogstad (as the villain), Dr. Ranks's confession of love, the damning letter in the mailbox and Nora's dancing of the Tarantella build the intensity to the climactic moment.

The heroine's fortunes depend on the conflict with the adversary. Nora's fortune wanes and waxes due to Krogstad's actions, specifically his blackmail, and then his retraction.

The obligatory scene, in which the central secret is revealed, simultaneously marks the lowest and highest points in the hero's fortunes. When Nora's secret is revealed to Torvald in Krogstad's first letter, Torvald's reaction brings Nora to her lowest point, surely solidifying her fears of losing her family and prompting her thoughts of suicide to save Torvald's reputation. However, when the second letter arrives and it is evident that Torvald no longer fears a destroyed reputation and forgives Nora for her actions, Nora realizes the truth about her marriage and decides to leave to discover herself, no longer desiring to exist as a doll or plaything for Torvald, empowering Nora to assert herself in a manner previously unattainable to her.

The denouement must be logical and credible. In this play, the denouement begins directly after Nora announces her decision to leave. The final moment of Nora closing the door behind her logically follows because Nora says she is leaving, and then she does so. Some readers have difficulties with the final scene of the play, disbelieving that Nora could change so rapidly. However, by carefully reading the script and paying close attention to the clues Nora leaves, her transformation appears to be logical and credible. Nora's awareness that she will not always be beautiful and that Torwald will not always look upon her as a plaything shows a tremendous amount of insight; likewise, when Torvald is able to change his mind so quickly when he receives the second letter, she realizes that everything she has built her life and dreams upon did not exist. She was contemplating killing herself for something that was not real. These are the reasons that support the assertive action Nora undertakes when she confronts Torvald before leaving the house.

For Further Reading:

Antonin Artaud. *Theatre and its Double.* New York: Grove Books, 1958.
James Roose-Evans. *Experimental Theatre: From Stanislavsky to Peter Brook.* New York: Routledge, 1996.
Jerzy Grotowski. *Towards a Poor Theatre.* London: Routledge, 2002.
Peter Brook. *The Empty Space.* London: Touchstone, 1995.
Roger Shattuck. *The Banquet Years: The Origins of the Avant-Garde in France.* New York: Vintage. 1968.

CHAPTER 11

BRECHT AND EPIC THEATRE

Bertolt Brecht und Helene Weigel am1.Mai, Horst Sturm, 1954

BERTOLT BRECHT (1898-1956) was one of the most distinguished representatives of socialist realist art. As a creator, he was multi-sided: poet, dramatist, director, critic and publicist. There can be little doubt that he was one of the most significant writers of the twentieth century. His work was the most important and original in European drama since Ibsen and Strindberg, but in many ways it is difficult to understand in itself and to relate it to a tradition which it at once develops and criticizes. Brecht had been writing continuously since 1918, however it was the period between 1937 and 1945 that saw not only some of his finest plays—*Mother Courage and Her Children, The Good Person of Szechwan,*

The Life of Galileo and *The Caucasian Chalk Circle*—but also the evolution of his most significant theories on the theatre.

Brecht's early dramas were anarchic, nihilistic and antibourgeois. In them, he glorifies antisocial outsiders such as fortune hunters, pirates and prostitutes; in keeping with their view on general society, the tone of these works is often cynical. In the years following his conversion to Marxism, Brecht wrote didactic plays whose style was austere and functional. These plays were intended to be performed in schools and factories by nonprofessional actors. In his later plays, Brecht combined the vitality of his early period with his Marxist beliefs to create plays that were dramatically effective, socially committed and peopled with realistic characters.

When Brecht began to formulate his ideas in the late 1920s, he had already experimented in a variety of techniques: he had written plays which showed the influence of the Expressionist trend in their loose construction, their treatment of the characters as types rather than individuals and their highly concentrated poetic language; and he had worked in close collaboration with Erwin Piscator (1893-1966, a German theatre director and producer), the exponent of the "political theatre" whose stage made use of every new technique in order to turn the theatre into a forum for the discussion of current affairs.

Berliner Ensemble Production of *Mother Courage and Her Children,* 1949

LAURIE J. WOLF

Brecht's theories show the impact of all of these experiments. He was convinced that the theatre must become a tool of social engineering, a laboratory of real social change:

> Today when human character must be understood as the "totality of all social conditions" the epic form is the only one that can comprehend all the processes, which could serve the drama as materials for a fully representative picture of the world.

Brecht wanted his theatre to intervene in the process of shaping society, a unique and monumental aspiration. He clearly did not believe that the existing theatre was capable of achieving this intention. He objected to the "theatre of illusion," as it was put forward in an essay titled "On Epic and Dramatic Poetry," authored by Goethe and Schiller in 1797. The salient section of the essay that Brecht objected to reads as follows:

> Thus the epic poet, the rhapsodic singer, relates what has happened in calm contemplation . . . he will freely range forward and backward in time . . . . The actor, on the other hand, is in exactly the opposite position: he represents himself as a definite individual; he wants the spectators to participate . . . in his action, to feel the sufferings of his soul and of his body with him, share his embarrassments and forget their own personalities for the sake of his . . . . The spectator must not be allowed to rise to thoughtful contemplation; he must not be allowed to rise to thoughtful contemplation; he must passionately follow the action; his imagination is completely silenced . . .

The thoughts put forward in this essay became the central issues of Brecht's theatrical perception. He believed that:

- Theatre is a dialectic, not the result of a dialectic—a dialect is a debate between two parties who hold differing views yet hope to come to the truth of the matter through the reasonable exchange of their perspectives.

- Theatre is a method of thinking, not a medium for presenting the results of thought.

- Theatre is a means used by societies to structure their experience.

- Theatre is exploratory and concerned with the activity of learning.

In order to achieve these goals, Brecht presented his theory of *verfremdungseffekt*. This is a theory that was derived from Russian Formalism as developed by Viktor Shklovsky and other Russian and Soviet writers and dealt with establishing the preciseness and independence of poetry and literature. In Brecht's hypothesis, frequently translated as *alienation effect*, he is actually encouraging his audience to take a metaphorical step back from the performance they are watching and reevaluate the form and content. He called his new form of theatre Epic Theatre, and there were very specific ways and means that *verfremdungseffekt* could be achieved.

The Marxist critic Walter Benjamin, a close friend of Brecht and one of his earliest champions, wrote about Brecht's Epic Theatre and explained further that art is a form of social production. He delineated very specific tenets about Epic Theatre that went quite some way toward clarifying the objectives that Brecht was attempting to realize; some of the major points follow:

- **Relaxed Audience**—A relaxed audience was more likely to be interested in and receptive to the playwright's message if they knew what was going to happen and were not looking ahead to the climax and conclusion.
- **Use of Fable**—Use of stories that are well known and familiar.
- **Untragic Hero**—Does not tend to come to blinding revelation about self; there is no tragic flaw or fall.
- **Interruptions**—Requires a constant refocusing of the audience's attention.
- **Quotable Gesture**—The actor has set of gestures, which convey social relations of character, and historical conditions, which make him behave as he does.
- **Didactic Play**—The play should be an austere apparatus; in theory, the actors and audience should be interchangeable, although in practice, this is not likely to happen.

Also, as written, Brecht tried to refuse to cultivate empathy—to which his audiences were accustomed.

- **The Actor**—The action happens in fits and starts, very comparable to cinematic images. Style is controlled by the dialectics of the scripts, e.g., songs and captions were used to differentiate scenes;

  - He would include interludes, which tended to destroy illusions;
  - The actor had to show event and also show her/himself *as* an actor;
  - There was to be no organic unity;
  - There was the use of readable signs (see Quotable Gesture).

- **Theatre on Public Platform**—Brecht wanted theatre to be viewed as if it was on a public platform; he believed in filling in the orchestra pit, in order to reduce the separation between the spectator and the play.

Brecht was not a fan of organic unity in a production; he wanted the seams to show. In other words, he never wanted his audience to forget they were in a theatre, watching a performance. He did not want them to sink into the stupor of complacency, but rather be active, participating members of the event. To this end, he wanted all of the trappings of the stage to be on display: lighting instruments, backstage areas and so forth. He believed that the play was never truly finished; it would resolve in an evening with a particular audience but that the content was always in a state of flux.

Brecht also observed how dramatic space is defined by four interrelated systems of signs:

- Placement and movement of characters in relation to each other and the audience.
- Objects seen on the stage or referred to in dialogue, including imagery.
- Abstract, fantastic or offstage constituted through dialogue.
- Architectural space of the real stage and theatre building in relation to its environment.

Brecht was also a dedicated follower of Marxism, beginning with his play, *The Mother*, written in 1932. Marxism is a scientific theory of human societies and the practice of transforming to them. It is the process of people trying to free themselves from certain forms of exploitation and oppression. The reason why Brecht was so taken with Marxism and why it is a viable form of literary criticism for us is because it is an analysis of literature in regard to the historical conditions, which have produced it. We are also able to examine the awareness that is present within literature itself of its own historical conditions.

Marxist criticism needs to be viewed as an active function when examining the significance of cultural and societal contexts. Its aim is to explain the work more fully, as is the intent of all literary criticism, but with Marxism, it pays particular attention to the works' forms, styles and meanings and views them as products of their own history. It works to facilitate the understanding of social relations between people and the way they produce their material life.

The forces and relations of production form the economic structure of society. The French Marxist philosopher Louis Althusser (1918-1990) wrote specifically about the ideology of society and what he referred to as State Apparatuses. He identified the "economic base," which he called the "repressive state apparatus." The economic base contains the different factions of government and has the responsibility of controlling where the finances of a country go and how they are to be used.

Althusser also distinguished the "superstructure" or the "ideological state apparatus." The superstructure legitimates the power of the social class that controls the economic base and is made up of forms of social consciousness (religious, ethical, educational) that are designated as ideology.

A Definition of Ideology

Ideology is the way people live out their roles in class society. It includes the values, ideas and images, which tie them to their social functions and so prevent them from a true knowledge of society as a whole.

In order to understand a particular ideology, it is essential to understand the precise relations of different classes in a society and where those classes stand in relation to the mode of production.

The superstructure of a society is an abstract; for that reason, it cannot form symmetry with the economic base; however, each element of the superstructure develops at its own rate, arising directly from the economic base. According to Althusser, "It is not the consciousness of a people that determines their being, but their social being that determines their consciousness."

Social relations between people are bound up with the way they produce their material life. In a true communist society, everyone contributes equally through labor. Despite this, is there a ruling class that has the greatest share of the wealth? And a much larger lower class whose labor supports the economic base collectively, but individually does not have any strength? This is an issue that Brecht addresses in his plays. Look for it in *The Good Person of Szechwan*.

Mallika Sarabhai in Bertolt Brecht's Indian adaptation of
The Good Person of Szechwan, directed by Arbind Gaur, Yodall, 2010

Brecht's relationship with women was and is one that remains controversial. There are numerous rumors even now, more than fifty years following his death, that the various women in his life had far more input into his writings than they were given credit for. Whoever wrote the bulk of his plays, there is no doubt that some of his female characters are among the strongest and most clearly articulated of his time period.

Frequently, his characters are single mothers whose motherhood has been variously established. Grusha from *The Caucasian Chalk Circle* has motherhood fall into her lap, when she rescues baby Michael from the revolutionary soldiers, but by the end of the play, he is decidedly her child, in this simulation of the King Solomon parable. Mother Courage's children all have different fathers, and the woman who is described within the play as "the hyena of the battlefield" could hardly be less motherly. For instance, when she is given the choice of selling her wagon or saving her son's life, she wavers so long that her son is killed. Hardly the mothering type.

Vlasova from *The Mother* shows a reinterpretation of the traditional role. Her journey through the play takes her from being an illiterate tea lady in a factory to becoming a well-educated leader in the Communist movement—a mother to the party.

What is interesting about these characters is that all are drawn from patriarchal thought, where nurturing is still restricted to a woman's sphere. The characters are defined by their mothering roles, or many of their actions result from the fact that they are mothers. All of them have lost their lovers or partners, either before the play begins or, in the case of Grusha, because of her actions in the play. The plays exclude desire and sexuality in favor of political content and function. Women tend to serve the central purpose of Epic Theatre because they are in a position, more so than their male counterparts, to reveal the societies they encounter. Because they are women, they tend to move outside of the circles of power, even within their own class, and therefore, are able to comment upon them.

Play for Study: Bertolt Brecht's The Good Person of Szechwan

Brecht sets up the problem of the play at the very beginning, which is the relationship between morality and the economic system, i.e., the impossibility of goodness under capitalism. How can Shen Te be good in a society that has forced her to become a prostitute in order to survive?

After the gods give her money to buy a tobacco shop, why does she create the persona of Shui Ta? The power that Shen Te derives from her disguise is obviously due in part to her construction as a man, however, on stage she is never simply a man. She is a female actor playing a woman playing a man (who occasionally forgets that she is a man). Brecht is addressing the fact that gender-related differences are associated more to the social expectations accompanying gender than to any natural differentiation by sex in psychological characteristics.

The representation of gender becomes even more complicated when Shen Te is pregnant; especially since pregnancy is one of the features traditionally associated with matriarchal power. With the exception of Mrs. Shin, the other characters assume Shui Ta is becoming fat as a result of his new wealth. As a result, we have an actor/character who is simultaneously reproducing and critiquing a construction that embodies both patriarchal and matriarchal power. The actor moves between and rejects two interwoven constructions of character, and by doing that, rejects fixing her character as one or the other.

Additionally, the play contains a subverted romantic plot, between Shen Te and Sun. Shen Te is shown as a woman who is trying to retrain her lover so that he might learn to be worthy of her desire. As a potential single mother, she maintains the major controlling factor in her own life, as well as that of her unborn child. Brecht conflates the private image of the expectant mother with the public figure of the woman/man as business magnate. This clarifies the differences between her role as a commodified woman and her cross-dressed self-authorship. We also learn that motherhood does not have to be the antithesis of sexuality, nor does it have to relegate the female character to selflessness.

By the end of the play, we are made to realize that the First God's project fails because Shen Te/Shui Ta must be viewed as an unstable, ever-changing subject. As Shui-Ta moves between an oppressive capitalism and a pragmatic, necessary self-love leading to the creation of self, each incarnation constantly looks at the other, and both confront the audience as it views them.

For Further Reading:

Augusto Boal. *Theatre of the Oppressed.* Charles A McBride, trans. New York: Theatre Communications Group, 1993.
Bertolt Brecht. *Brecht on Theatre: The Development of an Aesthetic.* John Willett, trans. New York: Hill and Wang, 1977.
Frederic Jameson. *Brecht and Method.* New York: Verso, 2011.
John Fuegi. *The Life and Lies of Bertolt Brecht.* New York: HarperCollins Publishers, Ltd., 1994.

CHAPTER 12

THEATRE OF DIVERSITY

THEATRE OF DIVERSITY has developed over the past thirty to forty years in order to increase awareness of discrimination and inequity in race, ethnicity, disability, gender, sexual orientation, aging and homelessness. More and more people in the United States are becoming aware of the multicultural and multiracial aspects of our society, although American culture used to pride itself on being the great "melting pot" that implied assimilation by all races and nationalities. In the past several decades, however, many previously marginalized groups in our society have encouraged that each group embrace and celebrate their difference, along with our shared principles.

This movement toward diversity has been, unsurprisingly, reflected in the theatre, with many organizations presenting special interest productions. These include a number of political, racial, ethnic and gender groups. This "performance of identity," which often includes autobiographical material, became one of the forms of theatrical activity that gives voice to individuals or groups who had been previously marginalized. A majority of the performances were less concerned with examining the character of the individual and more with the social, political and cultural context within which that individual functioned. The driving force of much of late twentieth-century theatre (and theatre of the past decade) is the attention paid to multiculturalism and postcoloniality. As performer and director, Philip Zarilli noted, "performance as a mode of cultural action is not a simple reflection of some essentialized, fixed attributes of a static, monolithic culture but an arena for the constant process of renegotiating experiences and meaning that constitute culture."

The rise of postcolonial theory opened other perspectives on cultural and political dimensions of performance, as performance came to represent not only the process of hegemonic political powers, but also the resistance to those powers. There is also the basic difference in thinking between practitioners and critics. Practitioners look for ways to perform the cultural differences they find personally and professionally stimulating; theatre critics frequently interpret these presentations of cultural border crossing as either neocolonialist or touristic. While the performance of one's ethnic or cultural heritage is often welcomed, the use of foreign or multiple cultures on the stage is generally looked at with mistrust. Therefore, while the representation of cultural traditions is praised, the crossing of cultural borders in performance is frequently looked on as inappropriate.

In defense of those who are dubious of crossing cultural borders in a theatrical event, it would not be unfair to say that many times the use of foreign cultures on the stage turns out to be a mere exoticization of the Other. These are the performances which at worst make superficial use of objects, masks or costumes from a different ethnic tradition, consequently fetishizing that culture, and at best perform music and movements that are devoid of appropriate training, and as a result, are nothing but the artist's imagination of who the Other is.

FEMEN Annual Protest Against Regular Summer Hot Water
Switch Off, Central Kiev, Ukraine 2010

When the women's movement began in the late 1960's, it existed in a very different sphere to the exhibition-oriented performance art work that was prevalent at the time. At the same time, many feminists were attracted to the structure of the performative situation that was in direct opposition to the dominant social systems of performance. In terms of modern feminism, this aligns most closely with materialist feminism, which looks specifically at the actual social apparatus or cultural practice that has produced them and to how this apparatus favors certain social interests rather than others. By the end of the 1980s, there was widespread interest among feminist performers and theorists internationally in the questioning, the exposing and the dismantling of those cultural and social constructions and assumptions that governed traditional gender roles, staging of the body and gender performance.

African American theatre was one of the earliest ethnic theatre movements. The founding of the Federal Theatre Project in the 1930s was intended to help artists through the Depression. There were units for African American performers in twenty-two cities, where they produced plays by both black and white authors. What was significant is that the Project made it possible to employ thousands of African American writers, actors, and designers, creating a new generation of theatre practitioners who would go on to develop the theatre of the 1940s and 1950s. There were several noteworthy plays during this period of time, such as *Native Son* by Richard Wright, directed by Orson Welles for his Mercury Theatre. Another important achievement was the performance of Paul Robeson as *Othello* on Broadway, which ran for 296 performances in 1943.

Probably the most important play of the postwar era was Lorraine Hansberry's *A Raisin in the Sun* (1959). It told the story of a Chicago family who planned to move into a white neighborhood but were finally convinced they were unwelcome. It was directed on Broadway by Lloyd Richards, the first African American director to do so.

Claudia McNeil in *A Raisen in the Sun* trailer, Columbia Pictures, 1961

LAURIE J. WOLF

From 1960 until the 1990s, there was a deluge of theatre by African American artist, much of which reflected the civil rights movement. In 1970, the Black Theatre Alliance listed more than 125 groups actively producing in the United States. Although only a handful of these survived the decade, many had a considerable influence. In addition to the emerging organizations, there was a growing attendance of African American theatregoers which accounted for a significant number of African American productions.

Theatre for Hispanic audiences has been thriving since Luis Valdez established El Teatro Campesino in San Juan Bautista in California. Hispanic theatre is actually divided into three groups: Chicano theatre, Cuban American theatre, and Puerto Rican theatre. The problem with Hispanic theatre at the current time is that there is not a force to set the wheels in motion to allow it to be produced. Playwright Caridad Svich, in writing about the problems, states:

> While the breadth and range of the work made by Latino theatre practitioners in the US is extraordinarily diverse in form and content and in geographic and regional specificity and historicization, our stages do not reflect this rich and abundant talent. High-profile houses slot a Latino play irregularly at best, and then often in the most provincial and patronizing circumstances. Our work is still viewed as the Other, as an exotic curiosity from an unknown, mysterious museum of human experience.

Although Svich paints a grim picture, there are still Hispanic playwrights writing and producing throughout the United States, including Svich herself. They include Luis Valdez (*Zoot Suit*), Maria Irene Fornes *(Fefu and Her Friends)* and Cherrie Moraga *(Giving Up the Ghost)*.

In addition to ethnic, class and sexuality differences, there are other axes of difference that Asian American scholars and artists have explored. Asian Americans encompass cultures as diverse as Chinese, Japanese, Korean, Filipino, Indian, Thai, Vietnamese or Cambodian. Minh-Ha T. Pham, in her doctoral dissertation, "Playing (with) Stereotypes: Comedy and Construction of Asian American Identities," examines the stereotype of the Asian American as a figure of fun and derision for the sake of comedy. To this end she states:

Comic race play exposes, exploits and pokes fun at the tension between, to adopt Frantz Fanon's phrase, the brown and yellow skin of Asian Americans, and the White mask required for cultural citizenship. Put another way, race play irreverently engages with the epistemic violence that, according to Fanon, splits racialized people from without (enacted through multiple processes of Othering) and from within (achieved by the internalization of self-as-other). The double movement of race play echoes Stuart Hall's helpful explication of "the double meaning of the metaphor" [play] as both describing performance and "permanent unsettlement." By playing (with) stereotypes, we are engaging in racial stereotypes that simultaneously destabilize hegemonic equations of power/knowledge that Others us from without and from within.

Two well-known Asian American companies are the East-West Players on the West Coast and the Pan Asian repertory on the East Coast. A number of plays by Asian Americans were produced in the 1970s and the 1980s. The most well-known of these was probably David Henry Hwang's *M Butterfly*, based on a true story about a French diplomat who falls in love with a singer from the Peking Opera Company, not knowing that he is actually a man, and lives with him/her for twenty years, in alleged ignorance.

There is no other group who has suffered cultural stereotyping as much as Native Americans, both onstage and in the cinema. Traditional Native American theatre tradition has been infused with rituals and religious celebrations, and customarily, there would not be a standard audience viewing the "performance." "In the 1970's, Hanay Geiogamah established the Native American Theatre Ensemble, which used western-type drama to express Native American values, traditions and aesthetics." However, at the moment, there is no generalized movement of Native American theatre. It is currently constrained from tribe to tribe. The ideal would be to eventually do away with old grudges and prejudices in order to create a more unified theatre movement, but there are years of history in the way.

Lesbian and Gay theatre, while usually combined into a single grouping, generally have separate agendas, but both are typically very politically oriented. During the 1990s, many Gay theatre companies focused on plays that dealt with the AIDS crisis. Lesbian theatre companies dealt with a wide range of topics, including power struggles and parental rights.

As you can see, the terms, social, cultural and political have become extremely important to the world of drama, theatre and performance. There are a myriad of considerations that must be factored in when producing a play or even reading a text for analysis. Try not to take anything for granted, but take into account as many outlooks as you can. The hints and techniques you have read about in this book have been just a beginning; there is a world of possibility for you to contemplate.

For Further Reading:

Bill Ashcroft, Gareth Griffiths and Helen Tiffin. *The Post-Colonial Studies Reader*. London: Routledge, 2008.
Homi Bhabha. *The Location of Culture*. London: Routledge, 1994.
Janelle G Reinelt and Joseph R Roach, eds. *Critical Theory and Performance*. Ann Arbor: University of Michigan Press, 1992.
Marvin Carlson. Performance: a Critical Introduction. New York: Routledge, 2004.

CONCLUSION

His Majesty's Theater Perth, Western Australia, 1932

THEATRE IS A remarkable alliance of artists, technicians, and spectators. It does not matter the size of the production; anytime a group of people work together toward a common purpose—whether it is a sporting event, an election, or coming together to support a cause—there is the sense of a shared achievement.

Theatre is the ultimate example of this experience. With the possible exception of opera, it is the most complex of the arts. A theatrical event goes through so many hands, and the contribution of each person is essential to its success.

Something that is truly unique about the theatre is that it is a survivor. It has been around for over 2,500 years and is still with us. It has withstood the test of time and other types of entertainment—television, movies, the Internet—and it still draws an audience. Part of the reason is that we are social creatures—we enjoy the exchange between the audience and the actors and between the audience members themselves. As long as people desire to join together to watch and appreciate representations of the human condition, the theatre will be there to provide it for them.

BIBLIOGRAPHY

Ackerman, James S. *Palladio: The Architect and Society*. Baltimore: Penguin Books Inc. 1966.

Aristotle. *Poetics*, James Hutton, trans., New York, W. W. Norton & Company, 1982.

Aronson, Arnold. *American Set Design*. New York: Theatre Communications Group, 1985.

Artaud, Antonin. *Theatre and Its Double*. New York: Grove Books, 1958.

Ashcroft, Bill, Gareth Griffiths and Helen Tiffin. *The Post-Colonial Studies Reader*. London: Routledge, 1995.

Austin, Gayle. *Feminist Theories for Dramatic Criticism*. Ann Arbor: University of Michigan Press, 1990.

Ball, David. *Backwards and Forwards: A Technical Manual for Reading Plays*. Carbondale: Southern Illinois University Press, 1990.

Barthes, Roland. *Empire of Signs*. New York: Hill and Wang, 1982.

Bay, Howard. *Stage Design*. New York: Drama Book Specialists, 1974.

Beadle, Richard. *The Cambridge Guide to Medieval Theatre*. Cambridge: Cambridge University Press. 1994.

Bellinger, Martha Fletcher. *The Commedia Dell'Arte*. New York: Henry Holt and Company, 1927. 8 December 2002 <http://www.theatrehistory. com/italian/ commedia_dell_arte_001.html>.

Benjamin, Walter. "The Task of the Translator." *Illuminations*. Hannah Arendt, ed. New York: Schoken Books, 1969.

Bentley, Gerald E. *The Professions of Dramatist and Player in Shakespeare's Time, 1590-1642*. Princeton, NJ: Princeton University Press, 1984.

Bhabha, Homi, ed. *Nation and Narration*. London, Routledge, 1990.

—. *The Location of Culture*. London: Routledge, 1994.

Boal, Augusto. *Theatre of the Oppressed*. Charles A McBride, trans. New York: Theatre Communications Group, 1993.

Booth, Michael R. *English Plays of the Nineteenth Century: Pantomimes, Extravaganzas and Burlesques*. Oxford: Oxford University Press, 1976.

Brecht, Bertolt. *Brecht on Theatre: The Development of an Aesthetic.* John Willett, trans. New York: Hill and Wang, 1977.

Brockett, Oscar and Robert Findlay. *Century of Innovation.* Boston: Allyn and Bacon, 1991.

Brook, Peter. *The Empty Space.* London: Touchstone, 1995.

Brubaker, David. *Court and commedia: The Italian Renaissance stage.* n.p.: R Rosen Press, 1975.

Bryce, Judith. *The Changing Scene: Plays and Playhouses in the Italian Renaissance.* Theatre of the English and Italian Renaissance. J. R. Mulryne and Margaret Shewring, eds. New York: St. Martin's Press, 1991.

Buck, Donald C., "Aesthetics, Politics, and Opera in the Vernacular: Madrid, 1737," *Opera Quarterly* (1994) 10(3): 71-91.

Cable, C. I. *Andrea Palladio: Biographical Highlights.* 18 November 1998.

—. *The Secrets of Palladio's Villas.* 18 November 1998.

Carlson, Marvin. *Performance: a Critical Introduction.* New York: Routledge, 2004.

—. *Places of Performance: The Semiotics of Theatre Architecture.* Ithaca: Cornell University Press, 1993.

Case, Sue-Ellen. *Feminism and Theatre.* New York: Methuen, 1988.

—. *Performing Feminisms: Critical Theory and Theatre.* Baltimore: Johns Hopkins University Press, 1990.

Clare, Janet. *Art Made Tongue-Tied By Authority: Elizabethan and Jacobean Dramatic Censorship.* Manchester: Manchester University Press, 1999.

Clurman, Harold. *On Directing.* New York: Collier, 1972.

Commedia Dell'Arte. 17 November 2002. 8 December 2002 <http:www.everything2. com/index.pl>.

Commedia Dell'Arte. December 2002, <http://math.bu.edu?INDIVIDUAL/jeffs/commedia.html>.

Counsell, Colin and Laurie Wolf. *Performance Analysis: an Introductory Coursebook.* London: Routledge, 2001.

De La Croix, Horst and Richard G Tansey. *Gardner's Art Through the Ages.* New York: Harcourt, Brace, Jovanovich, Inc., 1980.

De Lauretis, Teresa. *Technologies of Gender: Essays on Theory, Film, and Fiction.* Bloomington: Indiana University Press, 1987.

Elam, Keir. *The Semiotics of Theatre and Drama.* London and New York: Methuen, 1980.

Esslin, Martin. *Brecht: A Choice of Evils.* London: Methuen, 1984.

—. *The Theatre of the Absurd.* Middlesex: Penguin Books, 1961.

Evans, G Blakemore. *Elizabethan Jacobean Drama: The Theatre in Its Time*. New York: New Amsterdam Books, 1998.

Fraser, Russell A. and Norman Rabkin, eds. *Drama of the English Renaissance: The Tudor Period*. New York: Macmillan, 1976

Fuegi, John. *The Life and Lies of Bertolt Brecht*. New York: HarperCollins Publishers, Ltd., 1994.

Gassner, John. *Producing the Play*. New York: The Dryden Press, 1944.

Gates, Henry Louis, ed. *Black Literature and Literary Theory*. London: Methuen, 1984.

—. *The Signifying Monkey: a Theory of Afro-American Literary Criticism*. New York: Oxford University Press, 1988.

Georg II, Duke of Saxe-Meiningen (1826-1914), <u>Regisseur</u>, http://www. wayneturney.20m.com/saxe-meiningen.htm.

Gerould, Daniel, ed. *Theatre/Theory/Theatre: The Major Critical Texts from Aristotle and Zeami to Soyinka and Havel*. New York: Applause, 2000.

Giannachi, Gabriella and Mary Luckhurst, eds. *On Directing: Interviews with Directors*. New York: St Martin's Griffin, 1999.

Gilder, Rosamond. *Enter the Actress*. New York: Theatre Arts Books, 1931.

Gillette, A. S. *Stage Scenery: Its Construction and Rigging*. New York: Harper and Row, 1972.

Grimstead, David. *Melodrama Unveiled*. Chicago: University of Chicago press, 1968.

Grotowski, Jerzy. *Towards a Poor Theatre*. London: Routledge, 2002.

Hall, Stuart. *Resistance Through Rituals*. London: HarperCollins Academic, 1976.

Harrop, John and Sabin R. Epstein. *Acting with Style*. Boston: Allyn and Bacon, 2000.

Hayman, Ronald. *How to Read a Play*. New York: Grove Press, 1999.

Hewitt, Barnard, ed. The Renaissance Stage: Documents of Serlio, Sabbattini and Furtenbach. Coral Gables: University of Miami Press, 1958.

Hill, Christopher and Edmund Dell, eds. *The Good Old Cause: The English Revolution of 1640-1660*, London: Frank Case & Co., Ltd, 1969.

Hodge, Francis. *Play Directing: Analysis, Communication and Style*. Boston: Allyn and Bacon, 2000. hooks, bell (Gloria Watkins). "On Self-Recovery." *Talking Back: Thinking Feminist, Thinking Black*. Boston: South End Press, 1989.

Howarth, W. D. and Merlin Thomas, eds, *Molière: Stage and Study*, Oxford: The Clarendon Press, 1973.

Hume, Robert D. *The London Theatre World, 1660-1800*. Carbondale: Southern Illinois University Press, 1980.

Irelan, Scott, Anne Fletcher, Julie Felise Dubiner. *The Process of Dramaturgy*. Newburyport, Mass.: Focus Publishing, 2010.

Le Bon, Gustave. *The Crowd: A Study of the Popular Mind*. London: Benn, 1952.

Jameson, Frederic. *Brecht and Method*. New York: Verso, 2011.

Jones, Robert Edmond. *The Dramatic Imagination: Reflections and Speculations on the Art of the Theatre*. New York: Routledge, 2004.

Leacroft, Richard and Helen Leacroft. *Theatre and Playhouse*. London: Methuen, 1984.

Leggatt, Alexander. *English Drama: Shakespeare to the Restoration, 1590-1660*. London, Longman, 1988.

Levi-Strauss, Claude. *The Savage Mind*. London: Weidenfeld & Nicolson, 1972.

McAuley, Gay. *Space in Performance: Making Meaning in the Theatre*. Ann Arbor: University of Michigan Press, 2000.

McKendrick, Melveena. *Theatre in Spain, 1490-1700*. Cambridge: Cambridge University Press, 1989.

Maria, Salvatore Di. *The Italian Tragedy in the Renaissance: Cultural Realities and Theatrical Innovations*. Lewisburg: Bucknell University Press, 2002.

Marrapodi, Michele. *Italian Culture in the Drama of Shakespeare & his Contemporaries*. New York: Ashgate Publishing Company, 2007.

Mulryne, J R and Margaret Shewring. *Theatre of the English and Italian Renaissance*. New York: St Martin's, 1991.

Mulvey, Laura. "Visual Pleasure and Narrative Cinema." *Screen* 16, no. 13 (Autumn 1975).

Murray, Peter. *The Architecture of the Italian Renaissance*. New York: Schocken, 1997.

Palmer, Richard H. *The Lighting Art: The Aesthetics of Stage Lighting Design*. Boston: Allyn and Bacon, 1993.

Parker, W. Oren and R. Craig Wolf. *Scene Design and Stage Lighting*. Fort Worth, Tex.: Harcourt Brace, 1996.

Pavis, Patrice. *Theatre at the Crossroads of Culture*. Loren Kruger, trans. London: Routledge, 1992.

Pecktal, Lynn. *Costume Design: Techniques of Modern Masters*. New York: BackStage Books, 1999.

Pham, Minh-Ha T. "Playing (with) Stereotypes: Comedy and Construction of Asian American Identities," University of California, Berkeley, 2006.

Phelen, Peggy and Jill Lane, eds. *The Ends of Performance*. New York: New York University Press, 1998.

Pilbrow, Richard. *Stage Lighting Design*. London: Nick Hern Books, 1997.

Reinelt, Janelle G. and Joseph R Roach, eds. *Critical Theory and Performance*. Ann Arbor: University of Michigan Press, 1992.

Robinson, Alice M, Vera Mowry Roberts and Milly S Barranger, eds. *Notable Women in the American Theatre*. New York: Greenwood Press, 1989.

Roose-Evans, James. *Experimental Theatre: From Stanislavsky to Peter Brook*. New York: Routledge, 1996.

Rose, Martial, ed. *The Wakefield Mystery Plays*. New York: Doubleday and Company, 1963

Rowell, George. *The Victorian Theatre*. Cambridge: Cambridge University Press, 1978.

Russell, Douglas A. *Costume History and Style*. Boston: Allyn and Bacon, 1983.

"Theatre and Drama in the Nineteenth Century," *The Theatre of the Past*, n.p., n.d.

Said, Edward. *Culture and Imperialism*. New York: Alfred A Knopf, 1993.

—. *Orientalism*. New York: Random House, 1978.

Sauter, Willmar. *The Theatrical Event: Dynamics of Performance and Perception*. Iowa City: University of Iowa Press, 2000.

Serlio, Sebastiano. *The Book of Architecture 1611*. New York: Benjamin Blom, Inc. 1970.

Shattuck, Roger. *The Banquet Years: The Origins of the Avant-Garde in France*. New York: Vintage. 1968.

Smith, Winifred. *The Commedia Dell'Arte*. New York: Benjamin Blom, 1964.

Solomon, Alisa. *Re-Dressing the Canon*. London: Routledge, 1997.

Stern, Lawrence. *Stage Management*. Boston: Allyn and Bacon, 2000.

Styan, J L. *The Elements of Drama*. Cambridge: Cambridge University Press, 1960.

Svich, Caridad "Re-Mapping Latino Theatre: American Playwrights on the Edge of the Edge," *TheatreForum*, June 1 2005, 94-97.

Vince, Ronald W. *Ancient and Medieval Theatre*. Westport, Conn.: Greenwood, 1984.

—. *Neoclassical Theatre: A Historiographical Handbook*. New York: Greenwood, 1988.

Wainscott, Ronald and Kathy Fletcher. *Theatre: Collaborative Acts*. Boston: Pearson Education, 2004.

White, T. H. *The Age of Scandal*. Great Britain: Oxford University Press, 1950.

Williams, Raymond. *Drama from Ibsen to Brecht*. London: The Hogarth Press, 1993.

Wilson, Edwin. *The Theatre Experience*. New York: McGraw-Hill, 2001.

Wulbern, Julian H. *Brecht and Ionesco: Commitment in Context*. Urbana: University of Illinois Press, 1971.

Edwards Brothers Malloy
Thorofare, NJ USA
April 3, 2013